MW00783037

More
Secrets of
Hebrew Words

More
Secrets of
Hebrew Words

Holy Days and Happy Days

Rabbi Benjamin Blech

JASON ARONSON INC.
Northvale, New Jersey
London

This book is set in 11 pt. Cheltenham by Lind Graphics of Upper Saddle River, New Jersey, and printed by Haddon Craftsmen in Scranton, Pennsylvania.

10 9 8 7 6 5 4 3 2 1

Library of Congress Cataloging-in-Publication Data

Blech, Benjamin.
    More secrets of Hebrew words : holy days and happy days / Benjamin Blech.
      p. cm.
    English and Hebrew.
    ISBN 0-87668-223-9
    1. Fasts and feasts—Judaism—Miscellanea.   2. Gematria.
I. Title.
BM690.B52   1993
296.4′3—dc20
                                           93-14636

Manufactured in the United States of America. Jason Aronson Inc. offers books and cassettes. For information and catalog write to Jason Aronson Inc., 230 Livingston Street, Northvale, New Jersey 07647.

The greatest illusion
is to believe
that anything we do
is the result solely of our own efforts.

The *gematria* of
זֶה מַעֲשֵׂה יָדַי—this is the work of my hands—
is 451. It is the exact *gematria* of
לְהוֹדוֹת—to give thanks.
Achievement of any kind
necessitates acknowledgement and thanksgiving.

For making this volume possible,
I express gratitude to:

Arthur Kurzweil,
who first suggested to me the idea
for the initial volume
and who urged me to carry the project forward
with this sequel.
The Young Israel of Oceanside, my congregation,
whose appreciation of these ideas serves as a constant source
of inspiration and stimulation.
And most important of all—
my life-partner, Elaine;
my children: Tamar and Steven,
Yael and Stephen,
Jordana and Aryeh, and Ari;
and grandchildren Avital, Eitan, Talia, and Yair—
who make all of my days
holidays and *simhahs*.

Contents

Preface

The success of the first volume of *The Secrets of Hebrew Words* prompts this sequel.

Readers of the first work ranged from those who had the most rudimentary knowledge of Hebrew to rabbis and scholars. It was extremely rewarding for me to receive such enthusiastic response to a study of words that encompassed both the mathematical and the mystical, the most profound hidden meaning as well as the simple allusion implicit in a mere rearrangement of letters. The fear was that the intelligent layman, unfamiliar with the methodology of *gematria*, the study that treats Hebrew letters by way of their numerical meaning and finds relationships between words based on numeric equivalents, might reject out of hand any conclusions drawn from such a seemingly farfetched analysis. In the preface to the previous work, I already indicated how this system in Jewish thought long ago received the seal of approval from biblical and talmudic scholars. Even specific laws incumbent upon the Jewish people have their source in Torah allusions that rest solely on *gematria*. Compare the law that the נָזִיר (nazir) was to be in his state of holiness for precisely thirty days because the text says יִהְיֶה (YiHiYeH)—he shall be—and יִהְיֶה in *gematria* is 30: י = 10, ה = 5, י = 10, ה = 5 = 30 [*Nazir* 5a]. Perhaps even stranger to the uninitiated is the concept that words sharing identical letters have a common groundswell of meaning as well. The rearrangement allows for a difference of emphasis. The same letters, however, reflect a commonality of concept that often leads to fascinating ideas about some of the most fundamental principles within our faith.

Perceptive readers soon proved that I need not have worried. The mystical concept that God created the world with the letters and that they, therefore, formed the "atomic structure" of everything in the universe was quite readily recognized. The themes treated in the previously published *The Secrets of Hebrew Words* brought a wealth of fascinating insights and edifying information to the greater public.

This volume carries the selfsame approach further to an area that may be far more relevant. All of us share in the observance of holidays and happy days. The holidays are the יָמִים טוֹבִים (Yomim Tovim)—the festivals that comprise the annual cycle of the calendar year. The happy days are the special moments of our own lives that we share in a more personal way with family and friends—birth, בְּרִית (Brit), בַּר/בַּת מִצְוָה (Bar/Bat Miẓvah), and wedding.

The words identified with these days belong to the common vocabulary of almost everyone. Yet, their deeper meanings remain hidden for the most part. What they teach us remains unknown to those who cannot yet decipher the secrets of their profound language.

I invite you to take an eye-opening journey with me through the special days of the year—and the special days of your life. Perhaps you will be asked to speak or deliver words of blessing and congratulations at a שִׂמְחָה (simḥah). Perhaps you will be moved to share a word of Torah at your holiday table. Or perhaps you simply want to explore the beauties of a holy tongue which God used to write His Torah and whose secrets impart far greater meaning to every holy moment.

A יוֹם טוֹב (YOM TOV), a good day—a holiday or a happy day—in *gematria* is 73 (י = 10, ו = 6, מ = 40; ט = 9, ו = 6, ב = 2 = 73). That is the equivalent of the word כְּגַן (kegan), like a garden (כ = 20, ג = 3, ן = 50 = 73). We are no longer privileged to reside in the garden that God first created for us as paradise. Good days, however, are like that garden. If we probe their secrets, we can once again taste their precious fruits.

טַעֲמוּ וּרְאוּ כִּי־טוֹב יהוה (Ta'amu u-re'u ki-tov Adonai), Come taste and see that the Lord is good [Psalm 34:9].

A word about the method of transliteration used. We have adopted the Sefardic pronunciation. ח = ḥ. כ = kh. We have not differentiated between א and ע; both have been rendered as a. פ = f. צ = ẓ. Both כ and ק have been transliterated as k (not q for ק). The *sheva* (:) becomes e in Sefardic pronunciation (not i as in the Ashkenazic system). Ẓere (..) likewise is e in adherence to Sefardic custom; not ei as in the Ashkenazic community. Only where the vowel ẓere is followed by the letter *yod*, have we transliteraed it as ei. Thus *ben* for בֶּן, but *beit* for בֵּית.

A Note for Readers Who Don't Know Hebrew

You *can* gain a great deal from this book even if you don't (yet) know the Hebrew language.

Fundamental truths of our faith become abundantly clear as we study words for their rich philosophical and spiritual meanings. How we refer to things basically reflects how we comprehend their essence. Shakespeare may have been right: "And yet words are no deeds" [*Henry VIII*]. Nonetheless, they clearly are creeds—beliefs couched in the code of letters merged so as to have meaning on many levels.

Those conversant only with English may be somewhat surprised by the seemingly farfetched inferences, allusions, and even numerical correspondences suggested as credible explications. Yet even English has words that literate people recognize immediately as being composed not simply of letters, but rather serving as acronyms. The word "radar" no longer has periods after each letter to acknowledge its original source, but of course it comes from "Radio Detecting and Ranging." If someone unaware of the story behind the word were to be told that the radar can be related to a longer phrase of four words, that too would be farfetched. But ignorance of a word's parents does not justify mocking the parentage once it is revealed.

Hebrew comes with "secrets" far more numerous than the usage of acronyms. The most intriguing, perhaps, and the one often least acceptable to the western mind, simply because of unfamiliarity, is the code of *gematria*. It may appear as a mere game to take note of the fact that two totally different words, when translated into the language of numbers—for every Hebrew letter also bears a numerical equivalent—share the same total and hence have a relationship. The Hebrew word for child, ילד, for example is 44 (י = 10, ל = 30, ד = 4). Of course, that 44 is the sum of a father, אב (AV)—3 (א = 1, ב = 2) and a mother, אם (EM), 41 (א = 1, מ = 40). It is not simply man and woman, sperm and egg, that have merged; it is the numerical essence, the *gematria*, that is as powerful as genetics in the act of creation.

Gematria is simply a higher reality. When God created the original light of creation, את האור (et ha-or), its essence, not in terms of atoms and molecules, genes or chromosomes, but rather "letter numbers" was 613 (א = 1, ת = 400, ה = 5, א = 1, ו = 6, ר = 200 = 613). That light, as distinguished from sunlight, gave perfect clarity and understanding. So, too, would God later choose to give precisely 613 *mizvot* in His Torah. Equivalence of numbers bespeaks equivalence of meaning.

So, too, shared letters suggest shared meanings. If קבר (kever) means the grave, then how profound indeed that these same letters but slightly rearranged make the word בקר (boker), morning. The concept of immortality finds expression in the very word defining man's final resting place: the grave is but the "morning" of a higher form of existence.

Small children are soon taught that hydrogen, oxygen, and water have something in common. When water is written H_2O, we understand this relationship readily. *Gematria* teaches us what the "hydrogen" and "oxygen" components of every word really are.

Even *Halakhah*, the realm of legal categories, acknowledges the validity of numerical meaning. Concerning the *nazir*, the person who takes a vow of consecration unto the Lord to abstain from wine and strong drink, the Torah teaches: "All the days of his vow of Nazariteship, there shall no razor come upon his head; until the days be fulfilled, in which he consecrated himself unto the Lord, he shall be holy" [Numbers 6:5]. For how long does a *nazir* remain in this state of holiness? The text simply reads קדש יהיה (kadosh yiyeh). It is the Talmud [*Nazir* 5a] that deduces that the period of Nazariteship is for 30 days. How do we know? "Because the text says יהיה (yiyeh)—and יהיה (YiHYeH) in *gematria* is 30 (י = 10, ה = 5, י = 10, ה = 5)."

What you must know, however, to appreciate the "secrets" of this book are a few basics of Hebrew as they relate to letters:

1. Hebrew is almost always written without vowels. It is only consonants that appear in the Torah; vowels are self-understood in context.

A NOTE FOR READERS WHO DON'T KNOW HEBREW

2. For the purpose of *gematria*, only consonants are included for the numerical count.

3. There are two silent letters, the א and the ע, which receive their sound from accompanying vowels. They are, however, letters with numerical equivalents (א = 1; ע = 70) and they must always be counted when they appear.

4. There are two vowels, the "ō" and "ū" which may appear either as simple dots, in which case they have no numerical equivalent, or together with a ו (the dot over the ו turns it into "ō;" the dot inside the ו renders it "ū"). When the "ō" or "ū" have this ו for "support," the ו is counted as its usual number, that is, 6.

All this sounds far more difficult than it really is. Simply put, every letter that appears in a Hebrew text is also a number. That number is a message.

I promise you that the "secrets" are fascinating. Probe with me beneath the surface and uncover the hidden jewels of the Hebrew language that illuminate the truths of our faith, our values, our people, and our God.

Hebrew Alphabet, Transliterations, and Numerical Values

Hebrew Character	Name	Transliteration	Numerical Value
א	Alef	omit	1
בּ, ב	Bet, Vet	b, v	2
ג	Gimel	g	3
ד	Dalet	d	4
ה	He	h	5
ו	Vav	v	6
ז	Zayin	z	7
ח	Ḥet	ḥ	8
ט	Tet	t	9
י	Yod	y	10
כּ, כ	Kaf, Khaf	k, kh	20
ל	Lamed	l	30
מ	Mem	m	40
נ	Nun	n	50
ס	Samekh	s	60
ע	Ayin	omit	70
פּ, פ	Pe, Fe	p, f	80
צ	Ẓade	ẓ	90
ק	Kuf	k	100
ר	Resh	r	200
שׂ, שׁ	Sin, Shin	s, sh	300
ת	Tav	t	400

Part I

Holy Days

Chapter 1
שַׁבָּת
The Sabbath

זָכוֹר אֶת־יוֹם הַשַּׁבָּת לְקַדְּשׁוֹ

(Zakhor et yom ha-Shabbat le-kadesho)

שְׁמוֹת כ:ח

Remember the Sabbath day to keep
it holy.

Exodus 20:8

זָכוֹר, remember, begins with the letter ז,
which stands for the number 7:
Let every day of the week be directed
toward the seventh, the crown of creation,
the day on which the Lord had completed
all of His work and He rested.

Ba'al HaTurim, Exodus 20:8

SHaBaT

SABBATH

Three biblical laws are described in the Torah as "signs." Shabbat is a "sign":

בֵּינִי וּבֵין בְּנֵי יִשְׂרָאֵל אוֹת הִוא לְעֹלָם כִּי־שֵׁשֶׁת יָמִים עָשָׂה יהוה אֶת־הַשָּׁמַיִם וְאֶת־הָאָרֶץ וּבַיּוֹם הַשְּׁבִיעִי שָׁבַת וַיִּנָּפַשׁ

(Beini u-vein benei yisrael ot hi le-olam ki sheshet yamim asah Adonai et ha-shamayim ve-et ha-arez u-va-yom ha-shevi'i shavat va-yinafash)

"It shall be a sign for all time between Me and the people of Israel; for in six days the Lord made heaven and earth, and on the seventh day He ceased from work and rested."

[Exodus 31:17]

Brit, circumcision, is called a sign:

וּנְמַלְתֶּם אֵת בְּשַׂר עָרְלַתְכֶם וְהָיָה לְאוֹת בְּרִית בֵּינִי וּבֵינֵיכֶם

(U-nemaltem et besar orlatkhem ve-hayah le-ot berit beini u-veineikhem)

"You shall circumcise the flesh of your foreskin; and it shall be a sign of the covenant between Me and you."

[Genesis 17:11]

Third, and last, in this group of "signs" are the phylacteries, the *tefillin*:

וְהָיָה לְךָ לְאוֹת עַל־יָדְךָ וּלְזִכָּרוֹן בֵּין עֵינֶיךָ לְמַעַן תִּהְיֶה תּוֹרַת יהוה בְּפִיךָ כִּי בְּיָד חֲזָקָה הוֹצִאֲךָ יהוה מִמִּצְרָיִם

(Ve-hayah lekha le-ot al yadkha u-lezikaron bein einekha le-ma'an tihiyeh torat Adonai be-fikha ki be-yad ḥazakah hoẓi'akha Adonai mi-Miẓrayim)

"This shall serve you as a sign upon your hand and as a reminder on your forehead, in order that the law of the Lord may be in your mouth; for with a strong hand the Lord brought you out of Egypt."

[Exodus 13:9]

The three signs circumscribe the most fundamental beliefs of our faith: שַׁבָּת (Shabbat)—God created the world; בְּרִית (brit)—He continues the act of creation through our children; תְּפִילִין (tefillin)—He is involved in our history even as He took us out of Egypt.

שַׁבָּת (Shabbat), as the first of the set, is the most important and by way of acronym, all inclusive. Its three letters stand for

שַׁבָּת	(Shabbat)
בְּרִית	(Brit)
תְּפִילִין	(Tefillin)

SHaBaT

SABBATH

Yom Kippur, the Day of Atonement, is biblically described as *Shabbat Shabbaton*—"a Sabbath of Sabbaths" [Leviticus 16:31].

What do Shabbat and Yom Kippur have in common? One day a year, Jewish law demands that we set aside time for introspection, for self-analysis, for reevaluating our lives and our values. The goal of Yom Kippur, which comes as the last of the "Ten Days of Repentance," is *Teshuvah*. We must "return"—return to God and return to our inner core of spirituality rooted in our having been created "in the image of God."

That task cannot be accomplished on one day alone. Every week, after six days of secular life, we are to observe the mini-Sabbath of Sabbaths. The word *Shabbat* asks שַׁבְתָ (shavta)—did you return?

שַׁבָּת

SHaBaT

SABBATH

In the World-to-Come, says the Jerusalem Talmud, every person will be held accountable not only for sins committed, but pleasures of this world not enjoyed, physical delights not realized.

Asceticism is not the way of our faith. Body and soul are not in conflict; they must be harmoniously employed to serve the Creator.

Shabbat is a holy day. That is why we spend so much of it in prayer and in study. But we are also commanded to eat, to be happy, and, yes, there is even a great *mizvah* to refresh our bodies with sleep.

That is why the letters of Shabbat make reference by acronym to sleep:

שֵׁנָה	(Shenah) Sleep
בְּשַׁבָּת	(Be-Shabbat) on Shabbat
תַּעֲנוּג	(Ta'anug) is enjoyment.

Sleeping on Shabbat is fulfillment of "rejoicing."

SHaBaT

SABBATH

The first letter of Shabbat, the שׁ, is found at the entrance of every Jewish home. It appears on the *mezuzah* and refers to the name of God, *Shadai*.

That descriptive of the Almighty, *Shadai*, reminds us of the Creator's role as שׁוֹמֵר דַלְתֵי יִשְׂרָאֵל (**Sh**omer **D**altai Yisrael)—Guardian of the doorways of Israel.

God protects every Jewish household. And within every home, He places His agent: "בַּת" (bat)—daughter. The Jewish woman is given the role of bringing holiness into every house.

Six days a week, we work in the outside world. On the seventh we return to the inner palace of our families. It is the day of שׁ (Shadai) and בַּת (bat). The daughter of Israel, concerning whom it is said כָּל כְּבוּדָּה בַת־מֶלֶךְ פְּנִימָה (kol kevudah vat melekh penimah), "all glorious is the King's daughter within the palace" [Psalm 45:14], is the source of the sanctity of שַׁבָּת (Shabbat), the Sabbath.

שַׁבָּת

SHaBaT

SABBATH

The Torah begins with the word בְּרֵאשִׁית (bereshit), "in the beginning."

It introduces the story of creation. Superficially, it speaks in the language of narrative, rather than commandment.

Rearrange its letters, however, and note a striking reference:

יְרֵא שַׁבָּת = בְּרֵאשִׁית
(bereshit = yere Shabbat)
Revere the Sabbath

The first law alluded to in the Torah is the Sabbath, which, the Talmud Yerushalmi teaches, שְׁקוּלָה כְּנֶגֶד כָּל הַמִּצְוֹות (she-kulah ke-neged kol ha-miẓvot), "corresponds in importance to all other *miẓvot*" [*Berakhot* 1:5].

SHaBaT

SABBATH

Shabbat in time comes after six days not yet sacred. Shabbat in letters follows a word that forces us to "think" about its significance.

In the Hebrew alphabet, the letter before שׁ is ר; the letter before בּ is א; the letter before ת is שׁ.

The word רֹאשׁ (rosh), meaning head, comes right before שַׁבָּת (Shabbat). Consider the meaning of your days. Meditate upon the purpose of the seemingly secular and profane. Use your רֹאשׁ (rosh), your head, and you will "remember the Sabbath day to keep it holy" [Exodus 20:8].

נֵר

NeR

CANDLE

Two candles are lit to usher in the sanctity of the Sabbath.

נֵר (ner), the word candle, in *gematria* equals 250 (נ = 50, ר = 200). Two candles (2 × 250) are 500—the exact numerical equivalent of the first commandment given to mankind in the Bible, פְּרוּ וּרְבוּ (peru u-revu) (פ = 80, ר = 200, ו = 6 = 286 + ו = 6, ר = 200, ב = 2, ו = 6 = 214; 214 + 286 = 500).

For that reason there is an age old custom for the parents who accompany the bride and the groom as they walk down the aisle toward their canopy to hold a candle in their hands, the two candles together symbolizing the higher purpose of this union.

For Jews, sex is not sinful. To be creative is to imitate the Creator. Jewish law decrees: "Let the holy act be performed on the holy night."

The two candles gracing the Shabbat table mystically allude to the physical delights awaiting husband and wife, which are also a *miẓvah* of this holy day.

יַיִן

YaYiN

❦

WINE

We proclaim the holiness of Shabbat over a cup of wine.

יַיִן (YaYiN) the word for wine, in *gematria* is 70 (י = 10, י = 10, נ = 50 = 70).

There are שִׁבְעִים אֻמוֹת הָעוֹלָם (shivim umot ha-olam), seventy nations of the world [*Sukkah* 55b]. On the holiday of סוכות (Sukkot), we offer seventy sacrifices because after the introspection of the High Holy Days, our concern turns to the universal. A Jew does not think only of himself. Our dream is לְתַקֵן עוֹלָם בְּמַלְכוּת שַׁדַּי (le-taken olam be-malkhut Shaddai), "to perfect the world in the Kingdom of God" [Siddur, *Aleinu* prayer].

Wine is our way of emphasizing this obligation to all of mankind. Our weekly call to sanctification is associated with יַיִן (yayin)—the seventy nations of the world whom we must not forget in order to hasten the day when the Lord will be One and His Name will be One.

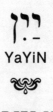

יַיִן

YaYiN

WINE

The Shabbat is compared by our sages to the "World-to-Come."

As the weekdays serve to prepare for the holiness of the Sabbath, so does our existence here on this earth serve as "corridor" to the life of eternity after death.

The biblical life span allotted to us is seventy years: "The days of our years are three score years and ten" [Psalm 90:10]. We make קִדּוּשׁ (kiddush) over יַיִן (yayin), wine, whose *gematria* is 70 (י = 10, י = 10, נ = 50 = 70) to symbolize our greatest obligation: Sanctify the seventy years of earthly existence in order to gain access to the spiritual bliss of Eternity.

דָּג
DaG

FISH

There is a specific food appropriate for the Shabbat meal.

דָּג (dag), fish, are a symbol of fertility. Their ability to multiply in great number is a sign of blessing. We pray we will be enabled to imitate them in some measure.

Shabbat, with its emphasis on the number seven, reminds us of the week of creation. Even as God created the world long ago, we must continue to re-create and to populate it.

The *gematria* of דָּג (dag) is 7 (ד = 4, ג = 3). The numerical meaning of this item on our menu for Shabbat recalls the time required for original creation and reinforces our link with the Creator Himself.

נֵר, יַיִן . . .

NeR, YaYiN . . .

CANDLE, WINE . . .

Five items characterize the Sabbath table: נֵר (ner) (candle), יַיִן (yayin) (wine), חַלָּה (halah), דָּג (dag) (fish), and בָּשָׂר (basar) (meat).

What they all have in common is their rootedness in the number 7, key to the week of creation.

Break these words into their digit sums and see the *gematria*.

Item	Letter *gematria*	*Gematria* sum	Digit sum
נֵר (NeR)	50 + 200 =	250	2 + 5 + 0 = 7
יַיִן (YaYiN)	10 + 10 + 50 =	70	7 + 0 = 7
חַלָּה (HaLaH)	8 + 30 + 5 =	43	4 + 3 = 7
דָּג (DaG)	4 + 3 =	7	4 + 3 = 7
בָּשָׂר (BaSaR)	200 + 300 + 2 =	502	5 + 0 + 2 = 7

Seven is the holiness of the Shabbat. Sanctify it with all those items that carry within them the seeds of Sabbath light, joy, pleasure, and happiness.

Mi-NeRah

FROM ITS CANDLE

From the light of a candle, we are able to dispel the darkness. מִנֵּרָה (mi-nerah), "from its candle," is the same as the word מְנֹרָה (menorah), the holy lamp that bore light in the Temple and from there to the world.

Take the letters in their fullness and add up their total: מֵם (MeM) (40 + 40 = 80), נוּן (NuN) (50 + 6 + 50 = 106), רֵישׁ (ReiYSH) (200 + 10 + 300 = 510), הֵא (HE) (5 + 1 = 6), for a total of 702.

Add the letters of the word שַׁבָּת (SHaBaT) (שׁ = 300, ב = 2, ת = 400 = 702).

From the candle in its fullness, with its rays reaching to all the corners of darkness, comes the same message as שַׁבָּת (Shabbat): The world will find peace, rest, and tranquillity because it was created by a good God, the Giver of light.

HaVDaLaH

SEPARATION

Shabbat ends with the prayer of the Havdalah. We must learn to distinguish between the sacred and the profane, the holy and the "not yet holy."

קִדּוּשׁ (kiddush) allows us to sanctify the Sabbath as it enters. הַבְדָּלָה (Havdalah) permits us to retain some of its splendor as we face the week to come.

When Rabbi Yochanan Ben Zakkai realized that the Temple would soon be destroyed, he pleaded with the Roman general: "תֵּן לִי יַבְנֶה וַחֲכָמֶיהָ" (Ten li Yavneh ve-ḥakhamehah) [*Gittin* 56b], "Give me the city of Yavneh and its wise men."

That school allowed Judaism to survive. Study replaced sacrifice as the medium for communication with the Almighty.

As we leave the Shabbat, equivalent to the Temple in its holiness, we, too, seek the spirit of Yavneh to insure our survival throughout the secular days of the week. For that reason, the Havdalah is comprised of four blessings:

יַיִן	= (yayin) wine
בְּשָׂמִים	= (besamim) spices
נֵר	= (ner) candle
הַבְדָּלָה	= Havdalah—the enumeration of the differences between holy and profane.

The first letters of these four blessings—the י, the ב, the נ, and the ה—form the word יַבְנֶה (Yavneh). We, too, will live, through the merit of Torah.

BeSaMiYM

SPICES

As Shabbat departs, we feel faint. We are losing our נְשָׁמָה יְתֵרָה (neshamah yeteirah)—the extra soul with which we have been blessed to study throughout the holy day.

Spices revive us because they remind us that we are not doomed to sin. When Adam and Eve first disobeyed the word of God, all four senses were involved in violations. They *listened* to the serpent, they lusted with their *eyes*, they *touched*, and they *tasted*. The sense of smell, however, remained pure. It did not rebel against God.

The word בְּשָׂמִים (besamim), spices, may also be read *ba-shamayim*, in the heavens. We are rejuvenated by the knowledge that we have maintained some of our heavenly essence. The spices revive us with their reminder of our heavenly potential.

עֹנֶג

ONeG

❦

REJOICING

שַׁבָּת (Shabbat) requires rejoicing. We are not simply obligated to observe; we must demonstrate through עֹנֶג שַׁבָּת (oneg Shabbat) that we love this *miẓvah* and acknowledge the Sabbath day as a foretaste of the time of messianic fulfillment.

וְנָהָר יֹצֵא מֵעֵדֶן לְהַשְׁקוֹת אֶת־הַגָּן
(Ve-nahar yoẓe me-Eden le-hashkot et-ha-gan)

God's original plan was for every day to allow us an existence of paradise. "A river went forth from Eden to water the garden."

[Genesis 2:10]

Eden, the river, the garden—these three would have spelled eternal bliss. The acronym for עֵדֶן (Eden)—Eden, נָהָר (nahar)—river, גָּן (gan)—garden, is עֹנֶג (oneg).

Because we sinned, we were cast out from the garden. But God did not destroy it. He merely expelled us and "He placed at the east of the Garden of Eden the Cherubim and the fiery revolving sword to keep the way to the Tree of Life" [Genesis 3:24].

The Garden of Eden and its river still exist. Someday, in the messianic era, we will be privileged to return. The עֹנֶג (oneg) of שַׁבָּת (Shabbat) reminds us of our dream—and our destiny.

SHaBaT

SABBATH

What is the foundation of Jewish life? What is the most important entity within the Jewish nation?

The first law given to the Jewish people was not to be fulfilled within the context of a large communal gathering. Instead the Jews were told: "In the tenth day of this month every man must take a lamb to a family, a lamb for each household" [Exodus 12:3].

It is within the home that a nation is born. It is from the family that a people emerges. Look carefully at the word שַׁבָּת (Shabbat). Central to it, in the very middle, is the letter ב, which means בַּיִת (bayit), house or home. Surrounding it are the שׁ and the ת, to make the word שֵׁת (shet), Hebrew for foundation. Every שַׁבָּת (Shabbat) we light candles in the home and reinforce our conviction that it is the center and the core of Jewish existence.

SHaBaT

SABBATH

Through תּוֹרָה (Torah), God speaks to us. It is His will made manifest. What it requires is human response.

The word תּוֹרָה (TORaH) in *gematria* is 611 (ת = 400, ו = 6, ר = 200, ה = 5 = 611). Without human assent, Torah remains nothing more than a heavenly ideal, a utopian charter.

It is mankind who must utter אָמֵן (Amen) to the Almighty's imperatives. The *gematria* of אָמֵן (AMeN) is 91 (א = 1, מ = 40, נ = 50 = 91).

Add אָמֵן (AMeN) to תּוֹרָה (TORaH), 91 to 611, and the total is 702. That is the *gematria* of שַׁבָּת (SHaBaT) (ש = 300, ב = 2, ת = 400 = 702). On שַׁבָּת (Shabbat) we testify to our belief in God and we acknowledge our acceptance of תּוֹרָה (Torah). It is the day blessed because תּוֹרָה (Torah) receives its acknowledgment of אָמֵן (Amen).

Chapter 2

רֹאשׁ הַשָּׁנָה

The New Year

בְּרֹאשׁ הַשָּׁנָה כָּל בָּאֵי הָעוֹלָם
עוֹבְרִין לְפָנָיו כִּבְנֵי מָרוֹן
שֶׁנֶּאֱמַר: הַיֹּצֵר יַחַד לִבָּם,
הַמֵּבִין אֶל־כָּל־מַעֲשֵׂיהֶם
[תְּהִילִים לג:טו]

(Be-Rosh Ha-Shanah kol ba'ei ha-olam ovrin le-fanav
ke-venei maron, she-ne'emar: "Ha-yozer yaḥad libam
ha-mevin el-kol-ma'aseihem")

מִשְׁנָה, רֹאשׁ הַשָּׁנָה א:ב

On the New Year, all creatures
pass before Him (God)
like children of Maron, as it says:
"He who fashions the heart of them all,
who considers all their doings"
[Psalm 33:15].

Mishnah, Rosh Hashanah 1:2

אֱלוּל

ELUL

ELUL

Rosh Ha-Shanah, the Jewish New Year, is preceded by the month of אֱלוּל. We know that we will be judged in the spirit of love and compassion. We do, after all, have a very special relationship with the Almighty.

שִׁיר הַשִׁירִים (Shir Ha-Shirim), the Song of Songs, is the paradigm for the way we relate one to another. God is the groom, we are the bride. Lover and beloved in their mutual passion best describe the Holy One and His people.

אֲנִי לְדוֹדִי וְדוֹדִי לִי (ani le-dodi ve-dodi li), "I am my beloved's and my beloved is mine" [Song of Songs 6:3]. That is how King Solomon, the wisest of all men, put it. Note the first letters of these four words conveying most intense feelings of love: ל, ו, ל, א. Together they form the word אֱלוּל (Elul).

We do not fear the Day of Judgment. The One who loves us as we do Him will find reason to judge us favorably.

אֱלוּל

ELUL

❦

ELUL

The month before Rosh Ha-Shanah demands that we begin our process of *teshuvah*, of repentance. Let us look back in retrospect and acknowledge our failings. Before we can set our feet on the correct path, we must acknowledge where we have gone wrong.

Read the word אֱלוּל (Elul) from back to front, with the insight of retrospect, and you discover two words—ל and ו = לוֹ (lo), to Him; ל and א = לֹא (lo), no, not.

To Him, to the Almighty who is the source of all goodness and the reason for our existence, we have all too often said "No." We did not heed His commandments. We did not follow His instructions. Recognition of sin is the first step on the road to repentance, says Maimonides. Once there is הַכָּרַת הַחֵטְא (hakarat ha-het), we may proceed to חֲרָטָה לְשֶׁעָבַר (haratah le-she'avar), remorse at our past misdeeds, followed by קַבָּלָה לְעָתִיד (kabbalah le-atid), acceptance of a new way for the future.

אֱלוּל

ELUL

ELUL

Søren Kierkegaard put it profoundly when he said:

"Life can only be understood backward; but it must be lived forward."

With the month of *Elul* we complete yet another year of our lives. To understand it, however, we must perceive it backward. That is the message of *Elul*.

Read it in reverse and it is a Hebrew word as well—לוּלֵא (lulei), were it not for. . . .

How different this year might have been were it not for . . . my foolishness, my rebelliousness, my insensitivity to fellow man, my immodesty and exaggerated sense of self toward God.

I look back, see how I have failed, and say לוּלֵא (lulei) . . . were it not for my failings, I could have achieved so much more. If, as Santayana says, "Those who do not learn from the past are condemned to repeat it," then I will be wiser. *Elul*, with the insight of "the backward look," will teach me to welcome the new year with a mind set that will ensure a כְּתִיבָה וַחֲתִימָה טוֹבָה (ketivah ve-ḥatimah tovah)—a year "written and sealed for goodness."

אֱלוּל

ELUL

ELUL

In the שְׁמוֹנֶה עֶשְׂרֵה (Shemoneh Esreh), the silent devotion recited three times every day, the central portion is devoted to בַּקָשָׁה (bakashah), requests for the most fundamental needs of life.

The very first of these requests asks for wisdom:

"Grant us knowledge, understanding and insight. Blessed are You, Lord, gracious Giver of knowledge."

Immediately following we plead:

"Cause us to return to You in perfect repentance. Blessed are You, Lord, Who desires repentance."

Only through knowledge can we arrive at *teshuvah*. Wisdom is the road that leads to true repentance.

The word בִּינָה (BiYNaH), understanding, in *gematria* is 67 (בּ = 2, י = 10, נ = 50, ה = 5). That, too, is the numeric value of אֱלוּל (ELUL) (א = 1, ל = 30, ו = 6, ל = 30). The בִּינָה (binah) of אֱלוּל (Elul) will allow us to attain the *teshuvah* required for the High Holy Days.

ELUL

ELUL

The prophet Amos cautioned his people: אַרְיֵה שָׁאָג מִי לֹא יִירָא (aryeih sha'ag mi lo yira), "The lion has roared. Who will not fear?" [Amos 3:8].

When God makes Himself manifest on this earth, can we possibly be immune to His message?

The roar of the Almighty takes many forms. He may be heard through events; He also speaks through the calendar as He proclaims, like a lion, אַרְיֵה (aryeih), the teachings of His holy days.

Note well the sequence of the יָמִים נוֹרָאִים (Yamim Nora'im), the Days of Awe:

אֱלוּל	Elul
רֹאשׁ הַשָּׁנָה	Rosh Ha-Shanah
יוֹם הַכִּפּוּרִים	Yom Kippur
הוֹשַׁעְנָא רַבָּא	Hoshanah Rabbah

Combine the first letters and the word אַרְיֵה (aryeih), lion, puts into perspective the forcefulness and the fear generated by these four divinely endowed moments.

רֹאשׁ הַשָּׁנָה

ROSH Ha-SHaNaH

THE NEW YEAR

When Jews were to be counted, God commanded Moses: כִּי תִשָּׂא אֶת־רֹאשׁ בְּנֵי־יִשְׂרָאֵל (Ki tisa et rosh benei Yisrael). Superficially the text is translated: "When you take a census of the children of Israel" [Exodus 30:12].

Literally, the meaning is far more profound: "When you lift up the heads of the children of Israel." To count the Jew is to make sure that he knows that he counts. And what makes a יִשְׂרָאֵל (Yisrael), an Israelite, so very special is that the word יִשְׂרָאֵל (Yisrael) has within it the letters that form לִי רֹאשׁ (li rosh)—to me there is a head, a mind. Created in the image of God, I have the ability to think and to study, to learn and thereby to fulfill the word of God. In the list of religious priorities: תַּלְמוּד תּוֹרָה כְּנֶגֶד כֻּלָּם (Talmud Torah ke-neged kulam), "The study of Torah takes precedence over them all" [*Shabbat* 127a].

That is why the first day of the year is called רֹאשׁ הַשָּׁנָה (Rosh Ha-Shanah). We acknowledge the head because from its directives, holy deeds will follow.

רֹאשׁ הַשָּׁנָה

ROSH Ha-SHaNaH

THE NEW YEAR

אַשְׁרֵי יוֹשְׁבֵי בֵיתֶךָ (Ashrei yoshevei veitekha), "Happy are they that dwell in Your house" [Psalm 84:5].

To live in the presence of God is to be assured of true bliss. אַשְׁרֵי (ashrei)—to be happy—is so much a biblical ideal that it is found in the first word of the Torah—בְּרֵאשִׁית (bereshit) (see the א, שׁ, ר, י) as well as in the last, יִשְׂרָאֵל (Yisrael) (again, note the א, שׁ, ר, י).

Hebrew words have three letter roots. אֲשֶׁר (asher)—when the א, the one, symbolic of one God, is the שַׂר (sar), the ruler over our lives—we may experience real happiness.

Rearrange those same letters and you have the word רֹאשׁ (rosh). Use the intellect God has given to you to understand His role in your life and you will be blessed with joy.

רֹאשׁ הַשָּׁנָה

ROSH Ha-SHaNaH

THE NEW YEAR

The Hebrew calendar follows not the sun, but the moon. The number of days in a lunar calendar year is 354.

The Hebrew word for year is שָׁנָה (shanah). In *gematria* it adds up to 355 (שׁ = 300, נ = 50, ה = 5).

How can we explain the discrepancy? Would it not have been far more correct if שָׁנָה (shanah) were, in fact, comprised of a total that accurately reflected its quantitative daily parts?

The answer imposes upon us a fundamental truth. All the days of the year, 354, are as nought if we do not add to them One, the awareness of *the* One who is both source and sustainer of time as well as the universe. Only if we comprehend a year as שָׁנָה (shanah), 355, can we pray for כְּתִיבָה וַחֲתִימָה טוֹבָה (ketivah ve-ḥatimah tovah), a year inscribed and sealed for good.

רֹאשׁ הַשָּׁנָה

ROSH Ha-SHaNaH

THE NEW YEAR

Long ago, Adam and Eve sinned. For that reason they were cast out of paradise.

We must strive for a new beginning, a רֹאשׁ (rosh), head, to the year that will hopefully change our destiny.

רֹאשׁ (ROSH) is an acronym for the three words that must serve as our motto:

רְצוֹן	Ritzon
אָבִינוּ	Avinu
שֶׁבַּשָּׁמַיִם	SHe-bashamayim

The will of our Father in heaven.

Following His commands rather than our desires will assure us of a year of blessing.

TiSHReY

TISHREI

The New Year begins with the month of תִּשְׁרֵי (Tishrei). Unlike נִיסָן (Nissan), which marks the birth of the Jewish people as we were taken out of the bondage of Egypt, תִּשְׁרֵי (Tishrei) commemorates the creation of the world.

The very first word of the Torah is בְּרֵאשִׁית (bereshit). Translated as "in the beginning," it designates no specific time for the formation of the heavens and earth. Rearranging these letters, however, gives us

בְּ	on
א	the first
תִּשְׁרֵי	of the month of תִּשְׁרֵי (Tishrei)

God has chosen the birthday of the world as most appropriate for annual review and judgment. That is why the astrological sign for the month is Libra, scales. We stand weighed at this time for all of our actions.

It is in תִּשְׁרֵי (Tishrei) that the letters rearrange themselves again and ask יָשַׁרְתָּ (yasharta)—have you acted properly?

מֶלֶךְ

MeLeKH

KING

רֹאשׁ הַשָׁנָה (Rosh Ha-Shanah) serves to proclaim God as King of the universe.

The שׁוֹפָר (shofar), trumpets His coronation. תַּשְׁלִיךְ (tashlikh), the ceremony where we go to a stream or a body of water, is in line with the custom that kings were crowned near the sea to show that their rulership extends over all the waters, to every land in the distance.

How do we know that God is indeed מֶלֶךְ (melekh), King of the universe? The letters of the word follow the Hebrew alphabet, but in *reverse order*. Sequentially, כ precedes ל, ל goes before מ. Seen in retrospect, they form מֶלֶךְ (melekh).

When Moses asked God, "Please let me behold Your glory" [Exodus 33:18], God responded: "You will see My Back, but My Face shall not be seen" [Exodus 33:23]. As events unfold, we do not grasp their significance. Living life day to day, we may not yet grasp the guiding Hand of God. With the perspective of retrospect, we perceive the wisdom of the Almighty. The letter ל, central to the word מֶלֶךְ, means learning and studying (לָמַד): Study the events of your life with the wisdom achieved by the "backward glance" ("You will see My Back . . . and you will truly acknowledge that God is King").

MeLeKH

KING

God judges us as King of the universe.

The word מֶלֶךְ (MeLeKH) numerically adds up to 90 (מ = 40, ל = 30, כ = 20). In Hebrew that is the letter צ (ẓadik), the very word meaning "righteous one."

Kings may be tyrants. Rulers may be dictators, uncaring and unjust.

Not so is God. צַדִּיק וְיָשָׁר הוּא (ẓadik ve-yashar hu), "just and righteous is He" [Deuteronomy 32:4]. Because we are judged by a King who is fair, we have no fear.

אָבִינוּ מַלְכֵּנוּ

AViYNU MaLKeiNU

OUR FATHER, OUR KING

On רֹאשׁ הַשָּׁנָה (Rosh Ha-Shanah) we stand before God in His dual role as parent and ruler.

He is our King with authority to do as He wishes. He is also our Father, personally concerned with our fate.

Combine the first letters of אָבִינוּ מַלְכֵּנוּ (Avinu Malkeinu) and note yet another allusion: א and מ joined together spell אֵם (eim), the Hebrew word for mother.

When a מִי שֶׁבֵּרַךְ (mi she-berakh), prayer for the sick, is offered in the synagogue, the name of the person for whom we pray is referred to by means of mother rather than father. Maternal love is called forth because it is so powerful. So, too, is God not only our Father, but also our Mother in Heaven.

Chapter 3
יוֹם הַכִּפֻּרִים
The Day of Atonement

שְׁחוֹרָה אֲנִי וְנָאוָה
[שִׁיר הַשִּׁירִים].
שְׁחוֹרָה אֲנִי כָּל יְמוֹת הַשָּׁנָה
וְנָאוָה אֲנִי בְּיוֹם הַכִּפּוּרִים

("Sheḥorah ani ve-navah" [Shir Ha-Shirim 1:5].
Sheḥorah ani kol yemot ha-shanah, ve-navah ani
be-Yom Ha-Kippurim)

שִׁיר הַשִּׁירִים רַבָּה א

"I am black and I am beautiful"
[Song of Songs 1:5].
I am black
throughout all the days of the year,
and I am beautiful
on the Day of Atonement.

Shir Ha-Shirim Rabbah 1

יוֹם הַכִּפֻּרִים

YOM Ha-KiPuRYM

THE DAY OF ATONEMENT

On the tenth of תִּשְׁרֵי (Tishrei) long ago, God finally forgave us for the sin of the Golden Calf.

To this very day, the tenth of תִּשְׁרֵי (Tishrei) possesses this unique power. Within it rests the capacity to secure atonement for our sins of the entire year.

It is יוֹם הַכִּפֻּרִים (Yom Ha-Kippurim). הַכִּפֻּרִים (Ha-KiPuRYM) in *gematria* is 355 (ה = 5, כ = 20, פ = 80, ר = 200, י = 10, מ = 40 = 355). That is exactly the same as the *gematria* of the word שָׁנָה (SHaNaH), year (ש = 300, נ = 50, ה = 5).

We pray with intense fervor because we know one day can indeed alter our fate for the entire year.

יוֹם הַכִּפֻּרִים

YOM Ha-KiPuRYM

DAY OF ATONEMENT

There is only one holiday in our calendar that contains the name of another within it.

יוֹם הַכִּפֻּרִים (Yom Ha-Kippurim) not only has פֻּרִים (Purim), within it, but can be translated as יוֹם (yom), a day, כְ (ke), like, פֻּרִים (Purim), the Festival of Lots.

The comparison is of course an anachronism. יוֹם הַכִּפֻּרִים (Yom Ha-Kippurim) is of biblical origin; פֻּרִים (Purim) is of much later rabbinic decree.

Yet there must be something to this striking comparison. Indeed, the key ceremony of the Day of Atonement revolves around casting lots: "And Aaron shall cast lots upon the two goats: one lot for the Lord and the other for Azazel" [Leviticus 16:8].

A lottery is God deciding, as He stands behind the scenes, which goat shall live, which goat shall die—the lottery determines their fate. But what seems like chance is the unseen Hand of God.

פֻּרִים (Purim) visibly demonstrated that coincidences were far more than coincidences. The gallows Haman prepared for Mordechai were really meant for himself. "On Yom Ha-Kippurim it is sealed: Who shall live and who shall die." The Day of Atonement is a day like פֻּרִים (Purim)—the lottery of life or death is the link between them.

יוֹם הַכִּפֻּרִים

YOM Ha-KiPuRYM

DAY OF ATONEMENT

כִּפֻּרִים (Kippurim) is a plural. It means atonements.

Why do we stress two types of atonement? Because sins come in two kinds, even as the Ten Commandments were written on two different tablets.

Five commandments—those on the first tablet—describe wrongdoings of man to the Creator. The five on the second tablet have as their subject wrongdoings of people to others.

Why, then, is this holy day so often referred to as יוֹם כִּפֻּר (Yom Kippur), in the singular? Because the *Mishnah* teaches us: "For transgressions between man and the Omnipresent, the Day of Atonement procures atonement, but for transgressions between man and his fellow, the Day of Atonement does not procure atonement until he has pacified his fellow" [*Yoma* 85b].

We must seek to achieve forgiveness for both types of sin. The day itself, however, only has power to undo the effects of one. It is we alone who can turn יוֹם כִּפֻּר (Yom Kippur) into יוֹם הַכִּפֻּרִים (Yom Ha-Kippurim) as we ask forgiveness from those whom we have harmed or hurt.

Ha-SaTaN

SATAN

The Jewish calendar is lunar. It nonetheless recognizes the greater accuracy of the solar and makes adjustments by means of seven out of nineteen year additions of leap months.

We use the moon to calculate time because it is a symbol of the Jewish people. It waxes and wanes, it has periods of light and of darkness, even as the Jewish people move in cycles from being compared to "the dust of the earth" to times when we are more like "the stars of the heavens."

We do know that the "real year" has 365 days (with but a slight adjustment necessary every four years). הַשָּׂטָן (Ha-Satan), Satan, has a role to play in this world. Although not possessing power independent of God, he is a messenger of evil who can cause harm to a Job or who can entice and ensnare mankind to evil. But his mission is limited by the numerical value of his name. הַשָּׂטָן (Ha-SaTaN) in *gematria* is 364 (ה = 5, שׂ = 300, ט = 9, נ = 50 = 364). On one day of the year, the day God designated for forgiveness and atonement, הַשָּׂטָן (Ha-Satan), Satan, is not allowed to engage in his work. On the Day of Atonement, when we are as angels, God dismisses the Devil.

סְלַח

SeLaH

❧

FORGIVE

God is our King. Rebellion against a king is punishable by death.

What allows us to turn to Him and plead סְלַח (selah)—forgive?

In *gematria* סְלַח (SeLaH) is 98 (ס = 60, ל = 30, ח = 8). That is precisely the *gematria* of לְבָנָיו (le-vanav) (ל = 30, ב = 2, נ = 50, י = 10, ו = 6 = 98).

Our relationship is made clear in the following verse:

בָּנִים אַתֶּם לַיהוה אֱלֹהֵיכֶם
(Banim atem l'Adonai Eloheikhem)

"You are the children of the Lord, your God."
[Deuteronomy 14:1]

He loves us as a parent. That is why we know we will be forgiven.

מָחַל

MeHaL

❦

PARDON

We need food in order to live. But the Bible teaches us:

כִּי לֹא עַל־הַלֶּחֶם לְבַדּוֹ יִחְיֶה הָאָדָם
(Ki lo al ha-lehem levado yihyeh ha-adam)

"Man does not live by bread alone."

[Deuteronomy 8:3]

Spiritual survival is at least as necessary as concern for the body. The letters for bread, לֶחֶם (LeHeM), when rearranged, become חלם (HaLoM), a dream. Indeed, as Friedrich Hebbel put it so well, "Dreams surely are for the spirit what sleep is for the body."

In dreams we aspire to what we have not yet been able to accomplish in deed. With Jacob, we see a vision of a ladder set on the earth, the top of it reaching to the heavens [Genesis 28:12]. We will aim higher; we will be better. For that reason, we dare also to dream that God will מָחַל (mahal), forgive.

The very same three letters betoken our three universal needs:

לֶחֶם	(lehem) for the sustenance of bread
חָלם	(halom) for the succor of dreams, and
מָחַל	(mehal) for the salvation of forgiveness.

Chapter 4

חַג הַסֻּכּוֹת
The Festival of Booths

בַּסֻּכֹּת תֵּשְׁבוּ שִׁבְעַת יָמִים כָּל־
הָאֶזְרָח בְּיִשְׂרָאֵל יֵשְׁבוּ בַּסֻּכֹּת.
לְמַעַן יֵדְעוּ דֹרֹתֵיכֶם כִּי בַסֻּכּוֹת
הוֹשַׁבְתִּי אֶת־בְּנֵי יִשְׂרָאֵל
בְּהוֹצִיאִי אוֹתָם מֵאֶרֶץ מִצְרָיִם
אֲנִי יהוה אֱלֹהֵיכֶם

(Ba-sukot teshvu shivat yamim kol-ha-ezraḥ be-Yisrael
yeshvu ba-sukot. Lema'an yed'u doroteikhem ki
ba-sukot hoshavti et benei Yisrael be-hoẓi'i otam
me-Ereẓ Miẓrayim Ani Adonai Eloheikhem.)

וַיִּקְרָא כג:מב–מג

You shall live in booths seven days;
all citizens of Israel shall dwell in booths,
so that your generations may know
that I made the children of Israel
live in booths when I brought them
out of the land of Egypt.
I am the Lord, your God.

Leviticus 23:42–43

SUKaH

BOOTH

The Hebrew word for the temporary hut in which we dwell on סוכּוֹת (Sukkot) is סֻכָּה (sukkah).

The three letters pictorially depict the kind of dwelling permitted by Jewish law in order to fulfill the מִצְוָה (miẓvah) of remembering the booths in which the Jewish people dwelt when they wandered in the desert.

The ס has four sides—the booth may be totally enclosed.

The כ has three sides and one total opening. That, too, is sufficient.

The ה has two "walls" and yet but a little more. The minimal requirement for a סֻכָּה (sukkah) is "two sides and a fraction."

סֻכָּה
SUKaH

BOOTH

The desert destroys. Without Divine intervention, no one can survive there.

When the Jews were delivered from Egypt, Passover merely marked redemption from human taskmasters. For forty additional long years, our ancestors had to face the harsh reality of cruel and uncaring forces of nature—bitter cold by night and blistering heat by day.

They survived through the miracle of "huts," protective clouds that surrounded them to demonstrate the truth of the words of the Psalmist that:

סוֹמֵךְ יהוה לְכָל הַנֹּפְלִים
(Somekh Adonai le-khol ha-noflim)

"The Lord upholds all that fall."

[Psalm 145:14]

סֻכָּה (sukkah) is the מִצְוָה (miẓvah) that commemorates this aspect of Divine care. The letters of the word סֻכָּה (sukkah) are an acronym for:

סוֹמֵךְ	(somekh) "upholding
כָּל	(kol) all
הַנֹּפְלִים	(ha-noflim) who fall."

SUKaH

BOOTH

The word סוּכָּה (sukkah) may be written with three letters or with four. The vowel can be placed under the ס or as the וּ. In the latter case, it is called מָלֵא (male), full or complete.

When man enters into the סֻכָּה (sukkah), the hut becomes "full," "complete."

The "full" סוּכָּה (SUKaH) adds up to a total of 91 (ס = 60, וּ = 6, כ = 20, ה = 5 = 91). That number is expressed in Hebrew as אֲצֵ, which aside from its numerical significance, also is the word *ze*, meaning "to leave" or "to remove oneself from."

To reside in the סוּכָּה (sukkah) for all the days of the holiday is "to leave" the confines of one's house and to acknowledge that true protection comes not from human-built walls, but rather from the Providential care of the Almighty.

אֲצֵ (*ze*), leave the protection of finite wood and stone; sit securely in the סוּכָּה (sukkah), whose safety is assured by the infinite Guardian of the universe.

סֻכָּה

SUKaH

❧

BOOTH

רֹאשׁ הַשָּׁנָה (Rosh Ha-Shanah) and יוֹם כִּפּוּר (Yom Kippur), both of which precede the festival of Sukkot, represent the two distinct aspects of the names used to describe God.

אֱלֹהִים (Elohim), God, is the descriptive used to convey the Almighty in His role as judge. It is the strict, stern, and demanding Father, grammatically bearing a masculine suffix (oi, im). That is God on רֹאשׁ הַשָּׁנָה (Rosh Ha-Shanah), called the יוֹם הַדִּין (Yom Ha-Din)—the "Day of Judgment." יהוה (Adonai), has a feminine ending (ה, ah). It refers not to the God of justice, but rather to the Lord of compassion. It stresses another dimension shared by the ruler of the world. יוֹם כִּפּוּר (Yom Kippur), the Day of Atonement, represents this side of Divinity—pardoning and forgiving out of great love and compassion.

Observing the High Holy Days expresses our understanding of these two aspects of the Almighty's essence. They are our "blessing." A blessing needs to be followed by the word אָמֵן (Amen), Amen, which means "I believe."

אָמֵן (AMeN) is 91 (א = 1, מ = 40, נ = 50 = 91). That is the numerical equivalent also of סוּכָּה (SUKaH) (ס = 60, ו = 6, כ = 20, ה = 5 = 91). I believe that God is both just and compassionate. That is why I entrust myself to His care and feel secure in the shelter of but a simple hut.

TeSHVU

YOU SHALL DWELL

בַּסֻּכֹּת תֵּשְׁבוּ שִׁבְעַת יָמִים
(Ba-sukkot teshvu shivat yamim)

You shall live in booths for seven days.

[Leviticus 23:42]

Throughout the year, the Jew feels most secure on the holy day of שַׁבָּת (Shabbat). It is the seventh day that on a weekly basis reminds us of the Creator.

The Sabbath is to remind us that "in six days the Lord made heaven and earth, the sea, and all that is in them, and rested on the seventh day" [Exodus 20:11] and also that "You shall remember that you were a servant in the land of Egypt, and the Lord, your God, brought you out of there by a mighty Hand and by an outstretched Arm" [Deuteronomy 5:15].

The seventh day commemorates not only that God created, but that He also continues to care.

On סֻכּוֹת (Sukkot) we are to experience that feeling of Providential concern, not just on שַׁבָּת (Shabbat), but on the six other days of the week as well.

Note the word תֵּשְׁבוּ (teshvu)—you shall dwell. It may be split into two parts: תֵּשֶׁב, you shall dwell, and ו, six—the six days of the week are in this instance to be transformed into a "Sabbath-type existence."

אֶתְרֹג

ETRoG

CITRON

וּלְקַחְתֶּם לָכֶם בַּיּוֹם הָרִאשׁוֹן פְּרִי עֵץ הָדָר

(U-lekaḥtem lakhem ba-yom ha-rishon peri eẓ hadar)

You shall take for yourself on the first day the fruit of goodly trees.

[Leviticus 23:40]

What is the "fruit of goodly trees?"

The only adjective given is הָדָר (hadar), the Hebrew word for beautiful.

What is beauty? John Keats said, "A thing of beauty is a joy forever." דּוֹר (dor) as a noun means "a generation." דָּר (dar) as a verb means "to reside, to remain for a lengthy period of time." הָדָר (hadar), beautiful, is composed of ה, "that which," דָּר, "is lasting, has permanence."

The biblical fruit alluded to must be the אֶתְרֹג (etrog), the only fruit הָדָר מִשָּׁנָה לְשָׁנָה (hadar mi-shanah le-shanah), which remains on the vine from year to year. Beauty is not the ephemeral or the transient. Constancy, in plants as well as in human beings, is the most important determinant of that which is truly desirable.

אֶתְרוֹג
ETROG

❧

CITRON

To be suitable as an אֶתְרוֹג (etrog), the citron used must be complete, whole, totally without blemish.

Four items in Jewish tradition always have attached to them the word שְׁלֵמָה (shelemah) to make clear that their efficacy is predicated upon their completeness:

1. אֱמוּנָה (emunah)—Belief

Maimonides prefaces each one of his thirteen basic principles of belief with the phrase אֲנִי מַאֲמִין בֶּאֱמוּנָה שְׁלֵמָה (Ani ma'amin be-emunah shelemah), I believe with perfect faith.

2. תְּשׁוּבָה (teshuvah)—Repentance

To qualify repentance is in fact to negate it. In our Silent Prayer we ask of God, וְהַחֲזִירֵנוּ בִּתְשׁוּבָה שְׁלֵמָה לְפָנֶיךָ (Ve-hahazirenu be-teshuvah shelemah le-fanekha), cause us to return to You in perfect repentance.

3. רְפוּאָה (refu'ah)—Healing

To be healed "just a little" is still to be sick. Our silent prayer adds וְהַעֲלֵה רְפוּאָה שְׁלֵמָה לְכָל מַכּוֹתֵינוּ (Ve-ha'ale refu'ah shelemah le-khol makoteinu), grant a perfect healing to all our ailments.

4. גְּאוּלָה (ge'ulah)—Redemption

Exile cannot come to an end with temporary havens. The messianic dream of our people is for גְּאוּלָה שְׁלֵמָה (ge'ulah shelemah), a complete and total redemption.

The אֶתְרֹג (etrog), plant symbol of beauty and wholeness, is an acronym for:

אֱמוּנָה	(Emunah) Belief
תְּשׁוּבָה	(Teshuvah) Repentance
רְפוּאָה	(Refu'ah) Healing
גְּאוּלָה	(Ge'ulah) Redemption

ETRoG

❧

CITRON

Plants are clearly dependent upon the Providential care of God.

The sun, the soil, the rain in its proper season, all must inter-eact to produce the harvest that the festival of Sukkot celebrates.

Pride makes the foolish believe they can prevail without Divine assistance. Alexander Pope put it well when he wrote:

Of all the causes which conspire to blind
Man's erring judgment, and misguide the mind,
What the weak head with strongest bias rules,
Is pride the never-failing vice of fools.

That is why the Psalmist prayed:

אַל־תְּבוֹאֵנִי רֶגֶל גַּאֲוָה
(Al tevo'eni regel ga'avah)

"Let not the foot of pride overtake me."
[Psalm 36:12]

Know that the first letters of those four Hebrew words spell the word אֶתְרֹג (etrog). The chief symbol of סוכות (Sukkot), Festival of the Harvest, serves to remind us of the need for humility.

ETRoG

CITRON

Four plants are used symbolically on סוּכּוֹת (Sukkot), the Festival of the Harvest.

First and chief amongst them is the אֶתְרֹג (etrog).

The numerical value of אֶתְרוֹג (ETROG) (full spelling) is 610 (א = 1, ת = 400, ר = 200, ו = 6, ג = 3 = 610). Add three other kinds to 610 and the total is 613.

613, our sages teach us, carries special significance: That is the total number of מִצְווֹת (miẓvot), Divine commandments, found in the Torah.

אֶתְרֹג
ETRoG

CITRON

Each one of the four plants commanded by God to be used on סוכות (Sukkot) represents a major organ of the body.

The אֶתְרֹג (etrog), as its shape indicates, is symbolic of the heart, in Hebrew called לֵב (lev).

Only the אֶתְרֹג (etrog) is given the descriptive "beautiful." Socrates said, "I pray O God, that I may be beautiful within." Beauty is not skin deep, but far deeper than the skin.

Beauty of a Jew is his heart, his inner essence. That, too, is what makes the Torah beautiful. Its last letter is ל, closing the final word, יִשְׂרָאֵל (Yisrael), Israel. Its first letter is ב, beginning the word בְּרֵאשִׁית (bereshit), in the beginning. Surrounding the Five Books of Moses is the word for heart. The plant that symbolizes the heart has the spotlight on the holiday that concludes with שִׂמְחַת תּוֹרָה (Simḥat Torah), rejoicing with the Torah.

לוּלָב

LULaV

PALM TREE

וּלְקַחְתֶּם לָכֶם בַּיּוֹם הָרִאשׁוֹן פְּרִי עֵץ הָדָר כַּפֹּת תְּמָרִים
(U-lekaḥtem lakhem ba-yom ha-rishon peri eẓ hadar
kapot temarim)

"You shall take for yourself on the first day the fruit of goodly trees, branches of palm trees. . . ."

[Leviticus 23:40]

The four plant species used on סוכות (Sukkot) are the אֶתְרֹג (etrog), the citron; the לוּלָב (lulav), the palm tree; הֲדַסִים (hadasim), the myrtle; and עֲרָבוֹת (aravot), the willow. Symbolically they stand for, respectively, the heart, the spine, the eyes, and the lips. All are brought together to share in praise of the Almighty.

The לוּלָב (lulav), as spine, reminds us not to bend or to cower in our allegiance to God. To be committed to a cause or to an ideal demands the "backbone" to stand up for our beliefs.

A wise person knows this message of the לוּלָב (lulav). לוּלָב (LULaV) in *gematria* is 68 (ל = 30, ו = 6, ל = 30, ב = 2 = 68). A wise man, a חָכָם (ḥakham), is also 68 (ח = 8, כ = 20, ם = 40 = 68).

Shakespeare had it correctly when he said:

Wise men ne'er sit and bewail their loss,
But cheerily seek how to redress their harms.
[Henry VI, Part III: Act V, Scene 4]

Fools prostate themselves before evil; the wise man stands tall and bends his knees to God alone.

LULaV

PALM TREE

The לוּלָב (lulav) is symbolic of the spine.

It reminds us to stand up with pride for what we believe in. It is the antithesis of the cringing Jew, the fearful Jew, the Jew who cowers in the presence of his enemies because he does not have sufficient faith in divine providence and protection.

What is the secret of the לוּלָב (lulav)? What gives the person with backbone the power to stand erect?

Look at the word לוּלָב (lulav). It divides into two shorter words: לוֹ (lo), to him, and לֵב (lev), heart.

The Jew who loves the Lord "with all his heart and with all his might" enjoys the fearlessness of his faith. For that very reason the לוּלָב (lulav) is joined to the אֶתְרֹג (etrog)—the symbols of spine and of heart are visibly related to each other.

לוּלָב

LULaV

❦

PALM TREE

In the Twenty-Third Psalm, King David told us how his faith removed fear and his confidence in God gave him life:

"Though I walk through the valley of the shadow of death, I will fear no evil, for You are with me."

[Psalm 23:4]

חַיִּים (ḤaYYiM), life, numerically adds up to 68 (ח = 8, י = 10, י = 10, מ = 40 = 68). That is the equivalent of the word לוּלָב (lulav) (ל = 30, ו = 6, ל = 30, ב = 2 = 68). Only those who stand up with pride for their convictions, and do not fear their countless enemies, may truly be said to be blessed with the gift of life.

Chapter 5

חֲנוּכָּה
The Festival of Lights

אִם כָּל הַמּוֹעֲדִים יִהְיוּ בְּטֵלִים,
חֲנוּכָּה וּפוּרִים לֹא נִבְטָלִים.

(Im kol ha-mo'adim yihyu betelim, Ḥanukah u-Purim
lo nivtalim)

תַּלְמוּד יְרוּשַׁלְמִי, תַּעֲנִית ב:ב

If all the holidays
will (in the messianic era) be nullified,
Chanukah and Purim
will not be nullified.

Taanit 2:2

HaNUKaH

THE FESTIVAL OF LIGHTS

Maccabees rededicated the Temple on the 25th of the Hebrew month of כִּסְלֵו (Kislev).

The word חֲנוּכָּה (Ḥanukkah) may be divided into two parts: חָנוּ (hanu)—they rested, כה (kah)—on the 25th (כ = 20, ה = 5).

The number 25 deserves its significant mention within the very name of the holiday. It is associated with light from the very time of creation. ראש הַשָּׁנָה (Rosh Ha-Shanah), on the first day of the month of תִּשְׁרֵי (Tishrei), marks the creation of Adam and Eve. That, of course, was the sixth day of the first week. Counting backward we see that the very first day, the day on which God proclaimed "Let there be light" [Genesis 1:3], was the 25th day of the preceding month, אֱלוּל (Elul).

Light came into being on the day of כה (kah), in *gematria* adding up to 25 and as a word meaning "thus": Through light we become enlightened; we see—and "thus" we comprehend.

חֲנוּכָּה (Ḥanukkah) miraculously merged the date of the rededication of the Temple with the time when the world was first granted the gift of a divine light lasting far longer than imaginable.

HaNUKaH

THE FESTIVAL OF LIGHTS

How many candles are to be lit on this Festival of Lights and in what order?

The school of Shammai and the school of Hillel, while agreeing that every night required a different number of candles with a maximum of eight, nevertheless strongly differed on the particular sequence. Shammai believed we begin on the first night with eight candles and progressively diminish the number until, on the last evening, there is to be lit only one. Symbolically, the message inferred is that although the spiritual light of Judaism survived, the passage of time makes it grow ever dimmer. Hillel was far more optimistic. The miracle of the Maccabees would not only be equaled, but even be exceeded in future generations. The light of Torah will burn ever brighter. The candles are to be lit in ascending order, from one to eight.

The very name of the holiday serves as acronym for our final decision.

ח	—	8
נֵרוֹת	—	(nerot) candles
וְהַלָכָה	—	(ve-halakhah) and the law is
כְּבֵית	—	(ke-veit) like the house of
הִלֵּל	—	Hillel.

HaNUKaH

THE FESTIVAL OF LIGHTS

The festival of חֲנוּכָּה (Ḥanukkah) demands פִּרְסוּמֵי נִיסָא (pir-sumei nisa)—publicizing the miracle. It is not enough to light the מְנוֹרָה (menorah) privately, to be seen merely by the members of our own household.

The threat to Jewish survival during the time of the Hasmonean Greeks came from the spirit of Hellenism. Even Jews who were not prepared to assimilate fully felt that, at most, religious identity could only be expressed among fellow Jews, but not in the outside world. "When in Rome, do as the Romans do" had its echo among those Jews who would never identify themselves as such publicly.

חֲנוּכָּה (Ḥanukkah) represents the miracle of the Hasidim over the Hellenists. We must be proud enough of the light of our faith and our tradition to publicize our belief. Note the message of the very letters that comprise the name of the holiday:

חוּצָה	—	(huẓah) outside
נִדְלָקִים	—	(nidlakim) are they lit
וּזְמַנָם	—	(u-zemanam) and their time
כָּל	—	(kol) all
הַלַּיְלָה	—	(ha-lailah) the night

Throughout all the times of darkness, we will not be ashamed to spread our light.

Ha-SHeMeN

THE OIL

On פּוּרִים (Purim) we feast. Our enemy then was Haman, who sought the physical destruction of the Jews. Genocide was his goal: "He sought to destroy, slay, and wipe out all the Jews, young and old, infants and women, in one day" [*Siddur, Al Ha-Nissim* prayer]. Because he did not succeed, our bodies rejoice; we eat and we drink.

חֲנוּכָּה (Hanukkah) commemorates a threat of a far different nature: "In the days of the Hasmoneans, Mattathias Ben Yochanan, the High Priest, and his sons, when a wicked Hellenic government rose against Your people Israel to make them forget Your Torah and transgress the laws of Your will" [*Siddur, Al Ha-Nissim* prayer]. Judaism, not the Jew, was the intended victim. The victory is a spiritual one; it is the soul of our people that offers thanksgiving.

Rearrange the letters of the word הַשֶּׁמֶן (ha-shemen), the oil, and you have the word נְשָׁמָה (neshamah), the soul. Rearrange the letters yet one more time and they make the word שְׁמוֹנֶה (shemoneh), eight. For eight days, the oil serves as symbol of the soul. Its light reminds us of the proverb of Solomon: "The spirit of man is the lamp of the Lord" [Proverbs 20:27].

Ha-SHeMeN

THE OIL

What kind of oil is to be used in the מְנוֹרָה (menorah)?

שֶׁמֶן זַיִת (shemen zayit), olive oil, is ideally required because it is the finest, the best quality to be found.

Cain and Abel both brought offerings to God. But the Torah teaches us that the Lord was pleased with only one of these gifts: "And the Lord paid heed to Abel and to his offering; but to Cain and to his offering He did not pay heed" [Genesis 4:4–5].

Why the difference of divine response? Because Cain brought "of the fruit of the ground" [Genesis 4:3]—of whatever came to hand. Abel, however, brought "of the firstlings of his flock and of the fat thereof" [Genesis 4:4]. Abel knew that what is set aside for God must be of the finest and the chosen.

The word שֶׁמֶן (shemen), oil, is an acronym for:

שֶׁמֶן	—	(shemen)	— oil
מִזַּיִת	—	(mi-zayit)	— from olives
נִבְחָר	—	(nivḥar)	— chosen

MaKaBiY

MACCABEE

A Jew knows he cannot simply sit back and wait for a miracle. Man must act together with the Almighty. Maccabee, a hammer, is a tool that indicates human involvement.

Who was the first to rally others round the cause of rededicating the Temple? The word מַכַּבִּי (Maccabee) is an acronym for the first hero of the חֲנוּכָּה (Ḥanukkah) story:

מַתִּתְיָהוּ	— Matityahu	—	Mattathias
כֹּהֵן	— Kohen	—	priest
בֶּן	— Ben	—	son of
יוֹחָנָן	— Yoḥanan	—	Yochanan

Because we were prepared to be the "hammer," God extended his mighty hand and performed miracles for us.

MaKaBiY

MACCABEE

When the Jews crossed the Red Sea after God had miraculously parted its waters for them, they sang a song of deliverance.

"Who is like You, O Lord, among the mighty?" [Exodus 15:11] was their rhetorical paean of praise.

Indeed, no one can compare to God. But Judaism stresses that we must strive to do so. Note the first letters of the four Hebrew words of their declaration:

מִי כָמֹכָה בָּאֵלִים יהוה
(Mi khamokha ba-elim Adonai)

Read the first letters together as word and they make מַכַּבִּי (Maccabee). When we fight evil and dedicate ourselves to the holy, we partake of the essence of the Almighty Himself.

מַתִּתְיָהוּ

MaTiTYaHU

MATITHIAS

מַתִּתְיָהוּ (Matityahu), Mattathias, sparked the revolt against the Greek rulers who had defiled the Temple.

חֲנוּכָּה (Ḥanukkah), the rededication of the spiritual center of the Jewish people, marked a new beginning. On a spiritual level, it was the equivalent of רֹאשׁ הַשָּׁנָה (Rosh Ha-Shanah).

The new year offers the opportunity to break with the past and to start spiritually fresh. The Temple cleansed of its idols and the מְנוֹרָה (menorah) relit allow for a new slate on the spiritual calendar of the Jewish people.

Note that the *gematria* of מַתִּתְיָהוּ (MaTiTYaHU) is 861 (מ = 40, ת = 400, ת = 400, י = 10, ה = 5, ו = 6 = 861). That is the exact numerical equivalent of רֹאשׁ הַשָּׁנָה (ROSH Ha-SHaNaH) (ר = 200, א = 1, שׁ = 300, ה = 5, שׁ = 300, נ = 50, ה = 5 = 861).

RaBiYM

MANY

The special prayer recited on חֲנוּכָּה (Ḥanukkah), the עַל הַנִּסִים (Al Ha-Nissim), thanking God for the miracles, emphasizes a major aspect of the victory of the Maccabees:

רַבִּים בְּיַד מְעַטִּים (rabim be-yad me'atim)—The many [were delivered] into the hands of the few.

This would not be the only time the Jewish people experienced a victory of this kind. Four major empires throughout the history of the world outnumbered us immensely, threatened us with extinction, and miraculously fell victim, רַבִּים בְּיַד מְעַטִּים (rabim be-yad me'atim), the many in the hands of the few.

Who are the רַבִּים (rabim)?

רוֹמִי	—	Rome
בָּבֶל	—	Babylon
יָוָן	—	Greece
מָדַי	—	Medea

חֲנוּכָּה (Ḥanukkah) teaches that just as the smallest of lights can defeat darkness, so can the smallest of people prevail over the greatest of empires.

HoSHeKH

DARKNESS

The threat we faced in the חֲנוּכָּה (Ḥanukkah) story is clearly described in the עַל הַנִּסִים (Al Ha-Nissim) prayer:

כְּשֶׁעָמְדָה מַלְכוּת יָוָן הָרְשָׁעָה עַל עַמְּךָ יִשְׂרָאֵל לְהַשְׁכִּיחָם תּוֹרָתֶךָ
(Ke-she-amedah malkhut Yavan ha-resha'ah al amekha
Yisrael le-hashkiḥam toratekha)

"When a wicked Hellenic government rose up against Your people, Israel, to make them forget Your Torah . . ."

[*Siddur, Al Ha-Nissim*]

Torah is compared to light:

כִּי נֵר מִצְוָה וְתוֹרָה אוֹר
(Ki ner miẓvah ve-torah or)

"For the commandment is a lamp and the Torah is light."

[Proverbs 6:23]

To forget the word of God is to be surrounded by darkness.

The Hebrew word for darkness is חֹשֶׁךְ (hoshekh). Rearrange its letters and you have שָׁכַח (shakhaḥ), forget.

Because our enemies sought to cause us the darkness of forgetfulness, we celebrate חֲנוּכָּה (Ḥanukkah) through the kindling of lights.

נ, ג, שׁ, ה

NUN, GiYMeL, SHiYN, HE

LETTERS ON THE DREIDEL

The game for חֲנֻכָּה (Ḥanukkah) is *Dreidel*. We spin a top, not knowing where it will land. The world turns, like the *dreidel*, and divine destiny determines what happens in the course of its spinning.

The four letters chosen to be on the four sides of the top are שׁ, ה, ג, נ. They stand for נֵס גָּדוֹל הָיָה שָׁם (nes gadol hayah sham), a great miracle happened there.

What seems like happenstance is history guided by God. It is He who has redeemed us when we were threatened in the very four ways alluded to by these self-same letters:

נ	—	נֶפֶשׁ	(nefesh)	—	the spirit
ג	—	גוּף	(guf)	—	the body
שׁ	—	שֵׂכֶל	(sekhel)	—	the intellect
ה	—	הַכֹּל	(ha-kol)	—	all of the above joined together

נ, ג, שׁ, ה

NUN, GiYMeL, SHiYN, HE

LETTERS ON THE DREIDEL

The challenge of the חֲנוּכָּה (Ḥanukkah) story was Hellenism and the threat of assimilation.

The miracle was that we survived in the face of an alien and seductive civilization.

The "light" of our faith, which by all natural law should have been extinguished and incapable of burning any longer, was somehow capable of sustaining an ever greater glow. That was the miracle of נֵס גָּדוֹל הָיָה שָׁם (nes gadol hayah sham)—a great miracle happened there—the first letters of which appear on the *dreidel.*

The first time a Jewish family ever faced a similar challenge was when the children of Israel were forced to settle in Egypt as a result of a famine. Jacob would not allow his sons to depart Israel until he had first created a separate district, a self-created ghetto, in the land of Egypt—a place the Bible calls the city of גֹּשֶׁן (Goshen). The Torah tells us:

וְאֶת יְהוּדָה שָׁלַח לְפָנָיו אֶל־יוֹסֵף לְהוֹרֹת לְפָנָיו גֹּשְׁנָה

(Ve-et Yehudah shalaḥ le-fanav el Yosef lehorot
le-fanav Goshnah)

"And he sent Judah before him to Joseph to show the way before him to Goshen."

[Genesis 46:28]

The letters in גֹּשְׁנָה (GoSHNaH)—to Goshen—are the very same letters that appear on the *dreidel,* proclaiming a miracle. Because we set ourselves apart and would not assimilate, we miraculously survived. גֹּשְׁנָה (GoSHNaH) in *gematria* is 358 (ג = 3, שׁ = 300, נ = 50, ה = 5 = 358). That is the secret of its numerical counterpart, the Hebrew word for Messiah, מָשִׁיחַ (MaSHiYaH) (מ = 40, שׁ = 300, י = 10, ח = 8 = 358).

MaSHiYaḤ

MESSIAH

How can we hasten the coming of the Messiah, מָשִׁיחַ (Mashiaḥ)?

We are called a מַמְלֶכֶת כֹּהֲנִים (mamlekhet kohanim), "a kingdom of priests" [Exodus 19:6]. What כֹּהֲנִים (kohanim), priests, are to the rest of the Jewish people, the Jewish people in entirety are to be to the remainder of the world.

Torah is light and we must enlighten all those who do not yet hear the word of the Lord. On חֲנוּכָּה (Ḥanukkah) we light candles. That is symbolic of our universal mission. For eight days we kindle the candles.

מַדְלִיקִין	—	(madlikin) we light
שְׁמוֹנָה	—	(shemonah) eight
יְמֵי	—	(yemei) days
חֲנוּכָּה	—	(Ḥanukkah) of Ḥanukkah

The first letters of these four words describing the מִצְוָה (miẓvah) of our lighting of candles spell the word מָשִׁיחַ (mashiaḥ), whose coming we hasten by this act.

Chapter 6
פּוּרִים
The Festival of Lots

מִשֶּׁנִּכְנָס אֲדָר מַרְבִּים בְּשִׂמְחָה
(Mi-she-nikhnas Adar marbim be-simḥah)

תַּעֲנִית כט

When the month of Adar enters,
we are due increased joy.

Taanit 29a

PURiYM

THE FESTIVAL OF LOTS

The hero of the פּוּרִים (Purim) holiday is a woman.

The special scroll recited on this day is מְגִלַּת אֶסְתֵּר (Megillat Esther). The book that tells us the story of the genocidal threat of Haman as well as God's miraculous deliverance is named after the heroine.

פּוּרִים (PURiYM) in *gematria* is 336 (פ = 80, ו = 6, ר = 200, י = 10, מ = 40 = 336). To whom are we grateful on this day? לְאִשָּׁה (Le-ISHaH), to a woman, the numerical total of which is identical to פּוּרִים (Purim), 336 (ל = 30, א = 1, שׁ = 300, ה = 5 = 336).

פּוּרִים

PURiYM

~~~

THE FESTIVAL OF LOTS

מְגִלַּת אֶסְתֵּר (Megillat Esther), the Book of Esther, is different in one respect from all other books of the Bible. It does not contain God's name even once.

God assuredly is not absent. He is merely hidden. He chooses to withdraw so that human beings might realize the responsibility they have to work together with God in bringing about miracles. Mankind must initiate; the Almighty promises that He will bring human effort to successful completion.

In the sacrificial system, as described in Leviticus (Chapter 23), the Jews were commanded to bring bullocks, symbolic of personal power and strength, to the Lord.

וּפָרִים (u-farim)—"and bullocks"—emphasizes the very idea behind the holiday that is called by these self-same letters rearranged: פּוּרִים (Purim). Esther and Mordechai could not wait for God to destroy Haman; God waited in the background to see if they understood that God helps those who help themselves.

PUR

LOT

Haman cast lots to determine the ideal date for the extermination of the Jewish people.

The singular of פּוּרִים (Purim) and the root word is פּוּר (pur). Every lot cast had as its intent "to destroy, slay and wipe out all the Jews, young and old, infants and women" [*Siddur, Al Ha-Nissim* prayer].

The פּוּר (pur) could not succeed. The very first מִצְוָה (miẓvah) given to mankind is the antithesis to this abhorrent "final solution." Immediately after creating Adam and Eve, the Torah tells us:

וַיְבָרֶךְ אֹתָם אֱלֹהִים וַיֹּאמֶר לָהֶם אֱלֹהִים פְּרוּ וּרְבוּ
(Va-yivarekh otam Elohim va-yomer lahem Elohim
peru u-revu)

"And God blessed them and God said to them, be fruitful and multiply."

[Genesis 1:28]

פְּרוּ (peru) is the decree of the Divine; the פּוּר (pur) of Haman is its perversion.

MeGiLaH

SCROLL

The מְגִלָּה (Megillah) is unique because the name of God does not appear within it.

Why does God choose to hide Himself?

The *gematria* of מְגִילָה (MeGiYLaH) (full spelling) is 88 (מ = 40, נ = 3, י = 10, ל = 30, ה = 5 = 88).

God withdraws on the stage of history in order to allow human beings to play a role. The *gematria* of וְעָבְדוּ (Ve-AVeDU)—"and *they* may serve"—is 88 (ו = 6, ע = 70, ב = 2, ד = 4, ו = 6).

"And they may serve" is the secret behind the seemingly strange feature of the מְגִלָּה (Megillah).

HaMaN

HAMAN

Haman is a descendant of the wicked tribe of עֲמָלֵק (Amalek).

The very first time עֲמָלֵק (Amalek) attacked the Jewish people— "Then came Amalek and fought with Israel in Refidim" [Exodus 17:8]—there was a reason why God allowed this to happen. The story followed immediately upon the verse: "And the name of the place was called Ma'aseh and Meribah because of the striving of the children of Israel, and because they tried the Lord, saying: 'Is the Lord among us or not?'"

Amalek may be the apparent enemy. The source of his power, however, is sin. It is God who must allow the attack of the anti-Semite.

הָמָן (HaMaN) in *gematria* is 95 (ה = 5, מ = 40, נ = 50). That is the exact equivalent of הַמֶּלֶךְ (Ha-MeLeKH), the King (ה = 5, מ = 40, ל = 30, כ = 20 = 95).

הָמָן (Haman) has power when the King Above decrees it.

HaMaN

HAMAN

After our ancestors left Egypt, they wandered in the desert for forty years.

How did they sustain themselves throughout all that time? What was the miraculous key to their survival? The Torah tells us:

וּבְנֵי יִשְׂרָאֵל אָכְלוּ אֶת־הַמָּן אַרְבָּעִים שָׁנָה עַד־בֹּאָם אֶל־אֶרֶץ נוֹשָׁבֶת
(U-venei Yisrael akhelu et ha-man arba'im shanah ad bo'am
el ereẓ noshavet)

"And the children of Israel ate the manna for forty years until they came to a land inhabited."

[Exodus 16:35]

הָמָן (ha-man), the manna, is the very name of our arch villain. What could they possibly have in common? All too often in Jewish history, it is only because Jews faced a common enemy that they found themselves able to unite. So, too, fear of one who sought to destroy us forced our people to turn back to God in prayer and submission.

What forty-eight prophets could not achieve, says the Talmud, was accomplished by the signet ring of הָמָן (Haman).

הָמָן (Haman), is sometimes as necessary for our survival as הָמָן (ha-man), the manna.

HaMaN

HAMAN

Why were the Jews in the days of אֲחַשְׁוֵרוֹשׁ (Aḥashverosh),
worthy of almost being annihilated?

The story of מְגִלַּת אֶסְתֵּר (Megillat Esther) begins with a party to
which all the people of his kingdom were invited. The feast featured
eating and drinking. Jews attended and, not wanting to appear
different, partook of the festivities. Because they were not concerned with כַּשְׁרוּת (kashrut) and ate what was forbidden to them,
the Talmud teaches that God allowed הָמָן (Haman) temporary li-
cense to threaten our people with extinction.

The very first time the letters of the name הָמָן (Haman) appear
in the Torah is when God castigates Adam and Eve after they
transgressed His first, and at that time only, commandment:

הֲמִן־הָעֵץ אֲשֶׁר צִוִּיתִיךָ לְבִלְתִּי אֲכָל־מִמֶּנּוּ אָכָלְתָּ
(Ha-min ha-eẓ asher ẓivitikha le-vilti akhal mimenu akhalta)

"Is it of the tree from which I commanded you not to eat that
you ate?"

[Genesis 3:11]

הֲמִן (Ha-Min)—"is it that"—is the name הָמָן (HaMan). Haman's
powers stem from our people's repeating the original sin of eating
"forbidden fruit."

עֲמָלֵק

AMaLeK

AMALEKITE

הָמָן (Haman) was an Amalekite.

עֲמָלֵק (Amalek) is the paradigm of all the persecutors of our people throughout the generations:

כִּי־יָד עַל־כֵּס יָהּ מִלְחָמָה לַיהוה בַּעֲמָלֵק מִדֹּר דֹּר
(Ki yad al kes yah milḥamah l'Adonai ba-Amalek mi-dor dor)

"The hand upon the throne of the Lord: The Lord will have war with Amalek from generation to generation."

[Exodus 17:16]

עֲמָלֵק (Amalek) has power over us only when we doubt the Almighty. The Hebrew word for doubt is סָפֵק (SaFeK). In *gematria* it equals 240 (ס = 60, פ = 80, ק = 100 = 240). That is the power of עֲמָלֵק (AMaLeK) (ע = 70, מ = 40, ל = 30, ק = 100 = 240). The Amalekite makes the Jew doubt his God—and that is how the Jew becomes vulnerable.

Chapter 7

פֶּסַח

The Festival of Freedom

כָּל שִׁבְעַת יְמֵי הֶחָג אָנוּ
קוֹרְאִים בָּהֶם אֶת הַהַלֵּל. אֲבָל
בַּפֶּסַח אֵין אָנוּ קוֹרְאִים אֶת
הַהַלֵּל אֶלָּא בְּיוֹם טוֹב הָרִאשׁוֹן
וְלֵילוֹ. לָמָה? מִשּׁוּם "בִּנְפֹל
אוֹיִבְךָ אַל־תִּשְׂמָח וּבִכָּשְׁלוֹ
אַל־יָגֵל לִבֶּךָ" [מִשְׁלֵי כד:יז]

(Kol shivat yemei he-ḥag anu kore'im bahem et
ha-hallel. Aval be-Pesaḥ ein anu kore'im et ha-hallel
ela be-yom tov ha-rishon ve-leilo. Lamah? Mishum
"binfol oyivkha al tismaḥ u-be-kashelo al yagel
libekha" [Mishle 24:17])

יַלְקוּט שִׁמְעוֹנִי, אֱמוֹר

All seven days of the festival (Sukkot)
we read the Hallel prayer,
but on Passover we do not read the Hallel
other than on the first day and its night.
Why?
Because "do not rejoice when your
enemy falls,
and let your heart not be glad when he
stumbles" [Proverbs 24:17]

Yalkut Shimoni, Emor

PeSaḤ

PASSOVER

The name of the festival of freedom, פֶּסַח (Pesaḥ), is a combination of two shorter words.

פֶּה (Peh) means mouth; סָח (Saḥ) means speaks. The severest aspect of servitude is the inability to speak out. The greatest freedom is freedom of speech, the right to say what one thinks without fear of reprisal.

On Passover night we became free and so we come together to recite the הַגָּדָה (Haggadah). We tell the story

וְכָל הַמַּרְבֶּה לְסַפֵּר בִּיצִיאַת מִצְרַיִם הֲרֵי זֶה מְשׁוּבָּח
(Ve-khol ha-marbeh lesaper biẓiyat miẓrayim harei
zeh meshubaḥ)

"And the more one relates concerning the Exodus, the more praiseworthy is he."

[*Haggadah*]

On פֶּסַח (Pesaḥ) we thank God for פֶּה סָח (peh saḥ), the ability of our mouths to speak freely.

חַג הַמַּצּוֹת

HaG Ha-MaZOT

THE FESTIVAL OF MAZOT

We became God's people on Passover.

It was then that we were commanded to make a festive meal and eat מַצּוֹת (mazot). Note that the word מַצּוֹת (mazot) can equally be read *mizvot*, commandments.

מַצּוֹת (mazot), one of the very first commandments given to the Jews, seems to be the paradigm for all מִצְוֹת (mizvot) of the Torah. What is its special feature? מַצּוֹת (mazot) must be watched carefully lest, with a minimal passage of time, they become leavened and forbidden.

מִצְוֹת (mizvot), just like מַצּוֹת (mazot), dare not be left undone. To delay the righteous act, to say that one has plenty of time to do it "tomorrow," is to render it as unfit as מַצּוֹת (mazot) turned sour through inattention and negligence.

MaẒaH

MAẒAH

On פֶּסַח (Pesaḥ) we must eat מַצָּה (maẓah); חָמֵץ (ḥameẓ), leavened bread, is forbidden.

The difference between חָמֵץ (ḥameẓ) and מַצָּה (maẓah) is not one of ingredients. Kosher and nonkosher foods are as different as cow and pig. But חָמֵץ (ḥameẓ) and מַצָּה (maẓah) are identical; חָמֵץ (ḥameẓ) is only מַצָּה (maẓah), just a little bit later. If the dough is allowed to rise and to leaven, it is no longer suitable, even if the smallest amount is involved.

Look carefully at the two words, חָמֵץ (ḥameẓ) and מַצָּה (maẓah). They, too, are almost identical. The מ and the צ are shared. It is only the ה and the ח that are different. Even these two letters are only unlike by the smallest of dots. If the foot of the ה rises, it becomes a ח. That, too, is when מַצָּה (maẓah) becomes חָמֵץ (ḥameẓ).

מַצָּה
MaZaH

MAẒAH

מַצָּה (maẓah) cannot be eaten alone.

מַצּוֹת יֵאָכֵל אֵת שִׁבְעַת הַיָּמִים
(Maẓot ye'akhel et shivat ha-yamim)

"Unleavened bread shall be eaten throughout the seven days."
[Exodus 13:7]

Not only are we required to eat מַצּוֹת (maẓot), but, as this text makes clear, we must see to it that others are enabled to eat of it as well. Our סֵדֶר (seder) begins with an invitation: "All those who are hungry, let them come and eat. All those who are needy, let them come and share the Passover with us."

The letter ו (vav) stands for "and"—it is referred to as the וָו הַחִבּוּר (vav ha-ḥibur), the ו (vav) that adds and attaches. Add a ו (vav) within the word מַצָּה (maẓah), and you get the word מִצְוָה (miẓvah). *Maẓah* shared is a *miẓvah* in the sight of God.

MaZaH

MAZAH

מַצָּה (mazah) is bread that has not risen.

מַצָּה (mazah) is "humble bread," lowly in stature. It serves to remind us of what we learned at the time of the Exodus:

כִּי בְּיָד חֲזָקָה הוֹצִיאֲךָ יהוה מִמִּצְרָיִם
(Ki be-yad ḥazakah hoẓi'akha Adonai mi-Miẓrayim)

"For with a strong hand the Lord took you out of Egypt."
[Exodus 13:9]

God is the source of everything that happens on this earth. A righteous person, a צַדִּיק (zadik), views events from the perspective of מֹשֶׁה (Mosheh):

וְנַחְנוּ מָה
(Ve-naḥnu mah)

"And what are we?"
[Exodus 16:7]

The word מַצָּה (mazah) has a צ at its center. The צ surrounds himself with the מ and the ה, the word מָה (mah). It is the thought that pervades his entire existence:

מָה אָנוּ מֶה חַיֵּינוּ
(Mah anu, meh ḥayeinu)

. . . . What are we, what are our lives. . . .
[*Maḥzor*, High Holy Day prayers]

שָׂאֹר

Se'OR

❦

LEAVENING AGENT

The forbidden foods of Passover are חָמֵץ (ḥameẓ) and שָׂאֹר (se'or). חָמֵץ (ḥameẓ) is leaven, bread; שָׂאֹר (se'or) is a leavening agent, yeast, something that has the capacity to make other items חָמֵץ (ḥameẓ).

Symbolically, the שָׂאֹר (se'or) represents those who pervert others. They are not so much the sinners, but those who cause others to sin.

They turn the "heads" of innocents. They mislead.

The word for head for Hebrew is רֹאשׁ (rosh). Look carefully at שָׂאֹר (se'or). It is to turn the head totally round.

HeRUT

FREEDOM

Passover is also known as זְמַן חֵרוּתֵינוּ (zeman heruteinu), the festival of our freedom.

The very first commandment teaches us how much God abhors slavery: "I am the Lord, your God, who brought you out of the land of Egypt, out of the house of bondage" [Exodus 20:2].

חֵרוּת (herut), freedom, was the goal of the Exodus. חֵרוּת (HeRUT) in *gematria* is 614 (ח = 8, ר = 200, ו = 6, ת = 400 = 614). That is the numerical meaning of the phrase הוֹצִיאָנוּ יהוה מִמִּצְרַיִם (HOZiYANU HaShem [YHVH] MiMiZRaYiM), the Lord took us out of Egypt (הוֹצִיאָנוּ: ה = 5, ו = 6, צ = 90, י = 10, א = 1, נ = 50, ו = 6 = 168; יהוה: י = 10, ה = 5, ו = 6, ה = 5 = 26; מִמִּצְרַיִם: מ = 40, מ = 40, צ = 90, ר = 200, י = 10, ם = 40 = 420) (168 + 26 + 420 = 614).

HeRUT

FREEDOM

Freedom is the necessary prerequisite to knowledge and understanding.

First came the festival of Passover, when the Jews left Egypt; then we came to Mount Sinai to accept the Torah, commemorated by the holiday of שָׁבוּעוֹת (Shavu'ot).

חֵרוּת (HeRUT) in *gematria* is 614 (ח = 8, ר = 200, ו = 6, ת = 400 = 614). The three kinds of intelligence in Hebrew are חָכְמָה (hokhmah), בִּינָה (binah), and דַּעַת (da'at)—wisdom, understanding, and knowledge. (It is interesting that the acronym for these three is the source of חַבַּ״ד [Habad], the Lubavitch movement.)

The combined numeric value of these three words is 614: חָכְמָה (HoKHMaH) (ח = 8, כ = 20, מ = 40, ה = 5 = 73). בִּינָה (BiYNaH) (ב = 2, י = 10, נ = 50, ה = 5 = 67). דַּעַת (Da'AT) (ד = 4, ע = 70, ת = 400 = 474). Added together, 474 + 67 + 73 = 614.

Freedom and true wisdom are inseparable.

HeRUT

FREEDOM

True freedom means I am free to be me.

Freedom is not to be cut off from one's source. A leaf that envies those unattached and seeks to be free of its branch as well as its sustaining root will, if given its wish, fly about aimlessly until it withers and dies. True freedom consists in the ability to choose an ideal cause to which one will be subservient.

When the Torah describes the Decalogue as חָרוּת עַל־הַלֻּחֹת (harut al ha-luhot), graven upon the tablets [Exodus 32:16], the Talmud comments, "Do not read חָרוּת (harut), graven, but rather חֵרוּת (herut) freedom. Obeying the Ten Commandments enables us to achieve the greatest freedom of personal integrity and fulfillment.

The Torah has 613 מִצְוֹת (mizvot), commandments. To add one, ourselves, to the yoke of the commandments is to get 614, the *gematria* of חֵרוּת (herut).

HaGaDaH

THE STORY

Evil is nothing other than good not yet comprehended.

Jewish law demands that just as we make a blessing over good things that happen to us, so, too, must we bless the "bad." A missed plane connection may seem bad for the moment; when the plane we did not catch subsequently crashes, that which appeared evil is now seen to be good.

The הַגָּדָה (Haggadah) is the story of our ancestors' journey from slavery to freedom. Even the slavery, however, had a purpose. It toughened us, it served as the "smelting pot" of the Jewish people to remove the dross and imperfections of those who otherwise would never have had to learn the lessons of overcoming hardships.

The הַגָּדָה (Haggadah) is the story of everything that was good. הַגָּדָה (HaGaDaH) in *gematria* is 17 (ה = 5, ג = 3, ד = 4, ה = 5 = 17. That is the number of the Hebrew word טוב (tov), good (ט = 9, ו = 6, ב = 2 = 17).

KOS

CUP

A cup of wine is used at the סֵדֶר (seder), to proclaim the greatness of God.

It is to fulfill the words of the Psalmist:

כּוֹס יְשׁוּעוֹת אֶשָּׂא וּבְשֵׁם יהוה אֶקְרָא
(Kos yeshu'ot esa u-ve-shem Adonai ekra)

"I will lift up the cup of salvation and call upon the name of the Lord."

[Psalm 116:13]

The *gematria* of כּוֹס (KOS) is 86 (כ = 20, ו = 6, ס = 60 = 86). That is the *gematria* of the name of God, אֱלֹהִים (ELoHiYM) in His role as Judge of the universe (א = 1, ל = 30, ה = 5, י = 10, מ = 40 = 86).

There are five cups at the Passover סֵדֶר (seder). Four are drunk by each of the participants and a fifth is poured out for Elijah. Every cup, כּוֹס (kos), is 86. And 5 × 86 = 430.

Note the biblical text: "Now the time that the children of Israel dwelt in Egypt was 430 years" [Exodus 12:40].

MaROR

BITTER HERBS

Slavery is bitter. מָרוֹר (maror), the bitter herbs, remind us of the time we suffered in Egypt.

But there is something even more bitter than being enslaved. מָרוֹר (MaROR) in *gematria* is 446 (מ = 40, ר = 200, ו = 6, ר = 200 = 446). That, too, is מָוֶת (MaVeT), death (מ = 40, ו = 6, ת = 400 = 446).

The bitterness of slavery prevented us from serving God. That, too, is the real tragedy of death:

לֹא הַמֵּתִים יְהַלְלוּ־יָהּ
(Lo ha-metim yehalelu-yah)

"The dead cannot praise the Lord."

[Psalm 115:17]

AViYV

SPRING

Passover is also known as חַג הָאָבִיב (Ḥag Ha-Aviv), the Festival of Spring.

In nature, trees begin to bud, flowers begin to blossom. In history, the Jewish people began to appear after a long "winter" of paganism and idolatry.

אָבִיב (aviv), the word for spring, readily breaks into two parts:

אָב (av) — father of
יב (yud-bet) — 12 — the 12 tribes of Israel

It is this month that witnessed the birth of a nation. It "fathered" a people divided into twelve distinct tribes, each blessed with unique gifts and talents, together sharing a commitment to one God and His will.

AViYV

SPRING

The New Year, רֹאשׁ הַשָּׁנָה (Rosh Ha-Shanah), begins with the month of תִּשְׁרֵי (Tishrei). That commemorates creation. It refers to the beginning of all mankind.

The Jewish calendar, however, marks another beginning as well. When God informed Moses and Aaron on the first day of נִיסָן (Nissan) that He would soon be redeeming His people, He said: "This month shall be for you the beginning of months; it shall be the first month of the year to you" [Exodus 12:2].

Two separate calendars interface one with another. Six months, beginning with תִּשְׁרֵי (Tishrei), precede the special New Year for the Jew. What שַׁבָּת (Shabbat) is to the six days preceding on a weekly basis, נִיסָן (Nissan) is to the months, bringing the sanctity of the Sabbath with the birth of the Jewish people.

This month is now אָבִיב (Aviv):

אָב (av)   — father of
יב (yud-bet) — 12 — the twelve months of the year.

Chapter 8
שָׁבוּעוֹת
The Festival of Weeks

בְּרִיךְ רַחֲמָנָא דִיהַב

אוֹרְיָאן תְּלִיתָאי

לְעַם תְּלִיתָאי

ע"י תְּלִיתָאי

בְּיוֹם תְּלִיתָאי

בְּיַרְחָא תְּלִיתָאי

(Birikh raḥamana diy'hav oryan telita'i le-am telita'i,
al yedei telita'i be-yom telita'i, be-yarḥa telita'i)

שַׁבָּת פח

Blessed be the Merciful One
Who gave a Torah of Three
(Five Books of Moses, Prophets,
and Writings)
to a people of Three
(Kohanim, Levites, and Israelites)
by means of Three
(Abraham, Isaac, and Jacob)
on day Three
("And let them be ready on the third day"—
[Exodus 19:11])
on the Third month
(*Sivan*, following the first month of *Nissan*
and then *Iyyar*).

Shabbat 88a

שָׁבוּעוֹת

SHaVU'OT

WEEKS

A week is a שָׁבוּעַ (shavu'a), from the root word שֶׁבַע (sheva), meaning seven.

Seven is the number identified with holiness. In six days God created the heavens and the earth, and on the seventh He rested. "And God blessed the seventh day, and hallowed it; because in it He rested from all His work that God in creating had made" [Genesis 2:3].

The highest level of holiness comes when seven is multiplied by itself. Seven times seven is 49.

שָׁבוּעוֹת (Shavu'ot) is nothing other than the fiftieth day after the Jews left Egypt. Forty-nine days, seven squared, they rid themselves of the impurities they acquired in a pagan and licentious world.

On the fiftieth day they were worthy of receiving the word of God at Sinai.

סִינַי

SiYNaY

❦

SINAI

At סִינַי (Sinai), God descended to give us His tablets and Torah.

Moses, however, had to ascend the mountain in order to receive this great gift. When man and God meet, both must make an effort. סִינַי (Sinai) connected the world below and the heavens above. Long before, Jacob had a dream in which he perceived that this linkage between heaven and earth was possible: "He dreamed that a ladder was set up on the earth and the top of it reached to heaven; and the angels of God were ascending and descending on it" [Genesis 28:12].

The Bible referred to the ladder as סֻלָּם (SuLaM). In *gematria* that is 130 (ס = 60, ל = 30, מ = 40 = 130). סִינַי (SiYNaY), too, shares in precisely that number (ס = 60, י = 10, נ = 50, י = 10 = 130).

Through the ladder of סִינַי (Sinai), mankind can climb to the very heavens above.

סִינַי
SiYNaY

SINAI

Why was the holiest mountain on which the Torah was given called סִינַי (Sinai)?

It was there that God first met מֹשֶׁה (Mosheh), when He appointed him to lead the Jewish people. "And the angel of the Lord appeared to him in a flame of fire out of the midst of a bush" [Exodus 3:2].

The bush was called סְנֶה (sneh). Its miraculous property was that although it was burning, it could not be consumed.

That would give the name to the mountain on which it stood. Because of the סְנֶה (sneh), the place was forevermore called סִינַי (Sinai). On it, the Jewish people received the Torah. Torah—the text given on that very spot where a bush could not be destroyed, although set ablaze—shares throughout all generations that miraculous attribute: no matter how often others have put the torch to our holy parchment, its message and its vision have not been consumed.

יִתְרוֹ

YiTRO

JETHRO

The סֶדְרָה (sedrah), the portion of the Torah in which revelation is recorded, is named after יִתְרוֹ (Jethro), father-in-law of Moses.

יִתְרוֹ (Jethro) was a convert to Judaism. He was not born into the faith. Precisely for that reason, he is singled out for this distinction—to emphasize that the Torah is meant for all mankind, not simply the descendants of Abraham, Isaac, and Jacob.

That is why on שָׁבוּעוֹת (Shavu'ot) the Book of Ruth is read. She, too, came from the pagan world to declare, "Your people shall be my people and your God, my God" [Ruth 1:16].

Non-Jews are also responsible for a minimal code of law, the seven universal laws of "the sons of Noah." רוּת (RUT) in *gematria* is 606 (ר = 200, ו = 6, ת = 400 = 606), because she willingly added unto her original seven responsibilities an additional 606 מִצְווֹת (miẓvot) to reach the biblically required total of 613. יִתְרוֹ (Yitro) shares the name רוּת (Ruth) for the same reason. He has in addition the י (yud), 10, to indicate the Ten Commandments given in the portion bearing his name.

דָּוִד

DaViD

DAVID

David was born on שָׁבוּעוֹת (Shavu'ot).

He was a descendant of רוּת (Ruth), the Moabite, who converted to Judaism. The king who wrote psalms stemmed from a woman not genetically Jewish, but, far more important, one who overcame the obstacles of an idolatrous past to voluntarily accept upon herself the yoke of the kingdom of Heaven.

דָּוִד (David) means beloved. In *gematria* דָּוִד (DaViD) is 14 (ד = 4, ו = 6, ד = 4 = 14). דָּוִד (David) was the fourteenth king of the Jewish people. Fourteen is also the Hebrew word יָד (yad), hand (י = 10, ד = 4). David would serve as the hand of God to draw people closer to the Almighty. His ancestor was the great convert, רוּת (Ruth). His descendant will be the Messiah, the one who will convert the entire world to the knowledge of God.

יְהוּדָה
YeHUDaH

JUDAH

David, born on שָׁבוּעוֹת (Shavu'ot), represents the beginning of kingship for the tribe of Judah.

On Jacob's death bed, he blessed his children and predicted their fate and their destiny:

לֹא־יָסוּר שֵׁבֶט מִיהוּדָה וּמְחֹקֵק מִבֵּין רַגְלָיו
(Lo yasur shevet miyhudah u-meḥokek mi-bein raglav)

"The scepter shall not depart from Judah nor the ruler's staff from between his feet."

[Genesis 49:10]

Messiah himself will come from the seed of David, of the tribe of Judah.

Note well the word יְהוּדָה (Yehudah). Within it is the holy four-letter name of God, יהוה. Added to it is a ד, the number 4. It is the role of יְהוּדָה (Yehudah) to see to it that the name of God be acknowledged throughout the four corners of the earth.

MiDBaR

DESERT

Speech is the measure of the greatness of mankind.

"God created man in His own image, in the image of God He created him" [Genesis 1:27]. What is "the image of God"? The תַּרְגוּם (Targum) commentary says "a speaking spirit."

The highest form of existence is to be a מְדַבֵּר (midaber)—one who speaks. The very same letters of מְדַבֵּר (midaber), with different vowels appended make the word מִדְבָּר (MiDBaR), desert.

The Torah was given in a מִדְבָּר (midbar) to show that it is mankind that has the choice between barrenness of desert or beauty of spoken word. The letters are the same; the decision is ours.

"I call heaven and earth to witness against you this day, that I have set before you life and death, the blessing and the curse; therefore choose life that you may live, you and you descendants" [Deuteronomy 30:19].

KoL

EVERYTHING

Is there really a person who has everything?

What then is everything? In Hebrew the word is כָּל (kol), all. In *gematria* it is 50 (כ = 20, ל = 30 = 50).

The Torah was given on the fiftieth day. That is Pentecost, שָׁבוּעוֹת (Shavu'ot). God said לְךָ (LeKHa)—to you (ל = 30, כ = 20 = 50). That is His gift to us. Understand the goodness of the Giver and His infinite wisdom and you know that the gift of the fiftieth day gives you כָּל (kol), everything.

ANoKHiY

I

God begins the Decalogue with the word אָנֹכִי (Anokhi):

אָנֹכִי יהוה אֱלֹהֶיךָ אֲשֶׁר הוֹצֵאתִיךָ מֵאֶרֶץ מִצְרַיִם מִבֵּית עֲבָדִים
(Anokhi Adonai Elohekha asher hoẓetikha me-ereẓ Miẓrayim
mibeit avadim)

"I am the Lord, your God, who brought you out of the land of
Egypt, from the house of bondage."

[Exodus 20:2]

The Torah itself began with the letter ב, the first letter of the
word בְּרֵאשִׁית (bereshit), in the beginning.

א precedes ב in the alphabet. אָנֹכִי (Anokhi), God, precedes
creation. אָנֹכִי (Anokhi), the introduction to law, comes before the
existence of the heavens and earth. Without God there would be no
world. Without Torah there would be no reason for the world to
exist.

ANoKHiY

I

God begins His address on Mount Sinai with the word אָנֹכִי (Anokhi).

Its four letters allude to the most significant numbers of our faith.

א	=	1	Sinai affirms there is only one God.
נ	=	50	Revelation of His word took place on the fiftieth day after the Exodus.
כ	=	20	Human beings are responsible in the heavenly court at age 20.
י	=	10	Responsibility is summarized in the Ten Commandments, which represents the categories for all 613 מִצְוֹת (miẓvot).

יוֹם הַשִּׁשִּׁי

YOM HaSHiYSHiY

THE SIXTH DAY

Every day of creation is referred to simply as day and number, e.g., "a fourth day, יוֹם רְבִיעִי (yom revi'i)" [Genesis 1:19], "a fifth day, יוֹם חֲמִישִׁי (yom ḥamishi)" [Genesis 1:23].

Not so the sixth. It is not יוֹם שִׁשִּׁי (yom shishi), but יוֹם הַשִּׁשִּׁי (yom ha-shishi); not a sixth day, but *the* sixth day.

To what does it refer? To the sixth day that justifies all of creation. The world came into being because of the Torah. The Torah would be given on the sixth day of סִיוָן (Sivan), the calendar date of שָׁבוּעוֹת (Shavu'ot). It is *that* sixth day that concludes the story of creation, even as it alludes to its goal and its purpose.

סְפִירָה

SeFiYRaH

COUNTING THE DAYS

When the Jews left Egypt they were told that seven weeks later they would be receiving the Torah at Sinai. God would lift the mountain over their heads, symbolic of a חוּפָּה (huppah), a wedding canopy, to convey the imagery that the relationship between our people and the Almighty is comparable to that between bride and groom.

So anxious were we for this moment of union that we began to count the days from the Exodus to Revelation. To this very day, the forty-nine days that separate פֶּסַח (Pesah) from שָׁבוּעוֹת (Shavu'ot) are the days of סְפִירָה (sefirah).

It is not merely days, however, that we count. The word סְפִירָה (sefirah) is made up of two shorter words: סֵפֶר (sefer), means book and יָה (Yah), is the name of God. The reason for counting is because we await the Book of God, the Torah given to us on the holiday of שָׁבוּעוֹת (Shavu'ot).

חָלָב

HaLaV

❧

MILK

On all other holidays, we are commanded to eat meat.

The Talmud teaches us: אֵין שִׂמְחָה אֶלָּא בְּבָשָׂר וְיָיִן (ein simhah ela be-vasar ve-yayin)—There is no true rejoicing except with meat and with wine [*Pesahim* 109a].

The holiday of שָׁבוּעוֹת (Shavu'ot) is different. Then we are enjoined to drink milk and to eat dairy products.

What is the significance of חָלָב (HaLaV)? In *gematria* it is the number 40 (ח = 8, ל = 30, ב = 2 = 40).

Forty days Moses spent on the top of the mountain. Forty days was the time required by God to transmit the truths of His divine law to His mortal messenger. Through the medium of "the forty" we to this day are blessed by knowing what God wants of us. Our meals are חָלָב (halav), dairy, to recall all that comes to us from that wondrous forty-day period.

חַג הַבִּכּוּרִים

HaG HaBiYKURiYM

FESTIVAL OF THE FIRST FRUITS

The holiday of שָׁבוּעוֹת (Shavu'ot) corresponds with the time when the first fruits in the fields have ripened. That is when the farmers were commanded to bring בִּכּוּרִים (bikurim), the first fruits, to Jerusalem.

What happens in nature coincides with the holiday's meaning in history. The Jewish people accepted the Torah on שָׁבוּעוֹת (Shavu'ot). God calls us בְּנִי בְּכֹרִי יִשְׂרָאֵל (beni bekhori Yisrael), "My son, my firstborn, is Israel" [Exodus 4:22]. Some day the whole world will proclaim God as King—"And the Lord will be King over the whole world, on that day the Lord will be One and His Name will be One" [Zechariah 14:9]. The uniqueness of the Jewish people rests primarily in being the בְּכוֹרִים (bekhorim), the first fruits, of the human family.

What is the reward for being the בְּכֹר (bekhor)—the firstborn? Re-arrange the letters of the word בְּכֹר (BeKHoR) and you get בֶּרֶךְ (BeRaKH), blessed. By accepting first that which other nations rejected, the Jewish people deserve the gift of special providential care and concern.

שָׁבוּעוֹת

SHaVU'OT

WEEKS

Without שָׁבוּעוֹת (Shavu'ot) there would be no other holidays. On שָׁבוּעוֹת (Shavu'ot) we received the Torah—and it is the Torah that gives us the laws, the obligations as well as the descriptions of all other festivals.

The word שָׁבוּעוֹת (Shavu'ot) has in it the word שֶׁבַע (sheva), seven. It is the key to all the other seven holy days that have their source in the Bible:

The first and seventh days of פֶּסַח (Pesaḥ) are יוֹם טוֹב (Yom Tov).

The first and seventh days of סוּכּוֹת (Sukkot) are יוֹם טוֹב (Yom Tov).

The eighth day of סוּכּוֹת (Sukkot), שְׁמִינִי עֲצֶרֶת (Shemini Azeret), is a holiday on its own.

רֹאשׁ הַשָּׁנָה (Rosh Ha-Shanah) is a holy day.

יוֹם כִּפּוּר (Yom Kippur) is a holy day.

The seven days of special sanctity all have their source in שָׁבוּעוֹת (Shavu'ot).

סְפִירָה

SeFiYRaH

COUNTING OF DAYS

Why could God not give us the Torah immediately after taking us out of Egypt? Why could the interim between Exodus and Revelation not be speeded up so that we might, at the earliest possible opportunity, be given the gift of God's word?

Forty-nine days had to pass and be counted. That was the time required for us to perfect ourselves and make ourselves worthy.

What is the most important attribute required by those who would become the bearers of God's message on earth?

The Sages, in *Ethics of the Fathers* 2:13, debated the matter: "He (Rabbi Yochanan ben Zakei) said to them: Go out and discern which is the proper way to which a man should cling. Rabbi Eliezer says a good eye. Rabbi Yehoshua says a good friend. Rabbi Yose says a good neighbor. Rabbi Shimon says one who considers the outcome of a deed. Rabbi Elazar says a good heart. He (Rabbi Yochanan ben Zakei) said to them: I prefer the words of Elazar ben Arach to your words for your words are all included in his words."

A good heart includes every other important trait. לֵב טוֹב (lev tov), is the foundation stone for ethical behavior. The *gematria* of לֵב טוֹב (LeV TOV) is 49 (לֵב = 32: ל = 30, ב = 2; טוֹב = 17: ט = 9, ו = 6, ב = 2). The סְפִירָה (sefirah) of forty-nine days preceding שָׁבוּעוֹת (Shavu'ot) is needed to inculcate within us the לֵב טוֹב (lev tov), the good heart, without which fulfillment of Torah law is impossible.

Chapter 9
תִּשְׁעָה בְּאָב
The Ninth of Av

עָתִיד הַקָּדוֹשׁ בָּרוּךְ הוּא לְהַפֵּךְ

תִּשְׁעָה בְּאָב לְשָׂשׂוֹן וּלְשִׂמְחָה

וּלְמוֹעֲדִים טוֹבִים וְלִבְנוֹת הוּא

בְּעַצְמוֹ אֶת יְרוּשָׁלַיִם

וּלְקַבֵּץ גָּלִיּוֹת

(Atid Ha-Kadosh Barukh Hu le-hapekh Tishah be-Av
le-sason u-le-simḥah u-le-mo'adim tovim ve-livnot hu
be-aẓmo et yerushalayim u-le-kabeẓ galiyot)

יַלְקוּט שִׁמְעוֹנִי, סוֹף אֵיכָה רַבָּתִי

God is destined to turn Tishah B'Av
to gladness and to joy
and to festivals of goodness,
and to build Jerusalem Himself
and to gather in the dispersed exiles.

Yalkut Shimoni, Eikhah, Rabati, end

תִּשְׁעָה בְּאָב

TiSHAH Be-AV

THE NINTH OF AV

Both Temples were destroyed on the identical date of the Jewish calendar.

Neither the Babylonians nor the Romans, more than half a millennium apart, particularly selected the Ninth of Av as the day on which they would put the Temple to the torch. Nor did they know that this very day many years before was the moment when the spies returned from their trip into Israel to report to the Jews in the desert that it would be impossible for them to come into the land and conquer it because "the land through which we have passed to explore it is a land that devours the inhabitants thereof; and all the people that we saw in it are giants" [Numbers 13:32]. It was then that God decreed: "You cry today for no reason. By your lives, in all the years to come I will give you cause to weep through punishments that will occur on this self-same day."

The Jews were expelled from Spain in 1492. When they looked at their calendars to see the day the queen had chosen to end the Golden Age of Spain, it was תִּשְׁעָה בְּאָב (Tisha Be-Av). When World War I broke out, in August of 1914, the exact day when hostilities began was once more the Ninth of אָב (Av).

אָב (Av) is not only the name of the month. It is the word that means father. The remarkable coincidences of history make clear that nothing is merely coincidence or happenstance. The events of אָב (Av) prove there is a "Father" in heaven. That, too, serves as consolation—for a Father will never allow the complete destruction of His children.

תִּשְׁעָה בְּ׳אָב

TiSHAH Be-AV

❦

THE NINTH OF AV

Every number has its special symbolic significance.

On Passover night, at the סֵדֶר (seder), we link numbers with a major idea to which they invariably correspond.

Who knows one? One is our God in the heavens and earth. Two are the tablets of the Decalogue. Three are the patriarchs, and four are the matriarchs. Five are the Books of Moses—the Written Law—and six are the sections of the מִשְׁנָה (Mishnah)—the Oral Law. Seven are the days of the week, and eight is the day of circumcision.

What is nine? Nine is the number the months of pregnancy. Nine is the number associated with the miracle of birth.

The very day associated with destruction contains within it the seed and the symbol of rebirth. Tradition teaches us that the Messiah will be born on the Ninth of אָב (Av). The day on which our people suffered so much is "pregnant" with the potential for final salvation.

תִּשְׁעָה בְּאָב

TiSHAH Be-AV

THE NINTH OF AV

The First Temple was destroyed on the Ninth of אָב (Av) in the year 586 B.C.E. The Second Temple was destroyed on the Ninth of אָב (Av) in the year 70 of the common era.

We weep and we mourn throughout the ages for this desecration of God's holy house. חוּרְבָּן הַבַּיִת (ḤURBaN Ha-BaYiT), as *gematria*, adds up to 683 (חוּרְבָּן: ח = 8, ו = 6, ר = 200, ב = 2, נ = 50 = 266; הַבַּיִת: ה = 5, ב = 2, י = 10, ת = 400 = 417; 266 + 417 = 683).

This had long ago been predicted by God when, in the aftermath of the false report of the spies, God decreed that this day would serve as the time for בְּכִיָה לְדוֹרוֹת (bekhiyah le-dorot), weeping for the generations. What is true weeping for the generations? Note its *gematria*: בְּכִיָה (BeKHiYaH) = 37 (ב = 2, כ = 20, י = 10, ה = 5 = 37), לְדוֹרוֹת (Le-DOROT) = 646 (ל = 30, ד = 4, ו = 6, ר = 200, ו = 6, ת = 400 = 646). 37 + 646 = 683.

The weeping of generations is justified as a response to the destruction of the Temple.

אֵיכָה

EYKHaH

LAMENTATIONS

On תִּשְׁעָה בְּאָב (Tisha Be-Av), Jewish communities around the world read the Book of אֵיכָה (Eikhah), Lamentations.

אֵיכָה (Eikhah), "How," is the first word as well as the name of the book in Hebrew. How, we ask, could You, the Almighty, have allowed this to happen? Divide the word into two and note a far deeper question: אֵי (Ei), where, כֹּה (koh), is the fulfillment of the word כֹּה (koh), which You promised us in the Torah:

וַיֹּאמֶר לוֹ כֹּה יִהְיֶה זַרְעֶךָ
(Va-yomer lo koh Adonai zarekha)

"And He said to him [Abraham]: Thus [like the stars] shall your descendants be."

[Genesis 15:5]

דַּבֵּר אֶל־אַהֲרֹן וְאֶל־בָּנָיו לֵאמֹר כֹּה תְבָרְכוּ אֶת בְּנֵי יִשְׂרָאֵל
(Daber el Aharon ve-el banav lemor koh tevarakhu et benei Yisrael)

"Speak to Aaron and to his sons saying, thus you shall bless the children of Israel."

[Numbers 6:23]

כֹּה (koh) is the key to our blessings. When Moses saw an Egyptian smiting a Hebrew the text tells us:

וַיִּפֶן כֹּה וָכֹה
(Va-yifen koh va-khoh)

"And he looked this way and that way [for the כֹּה (koh) and the כֹּה (koh)]."

[Exodus 2:12]

HOLY DAYS

Moses wondered most of all what happened to God's promise of blessing introduced with the word כֹּה (koh).

That is what we ask of God as well when we contemplate our national tragedies: אֵיכָה (Eikhah), אֵי (Ei), where, כֹּה (koh), are the blessings of כֹּה (koh)?

EYKHaH

LAMENTATIONS

The same word, when understood on a more profound level, serves as both question and answer to the problem of our people's catastrophes.

אֵיכָה (Eikhah) is the plaint we place before God: How? How could you do this to us, O God? How could you allow our enemies to humiliate us so and to destroy our most sacred possession?

Ironic, indeed, that we use the very word that, with different vowels, is the accusation flung at the first man by God when he transgressed in the Garden of Eden:

וַיִּקְרָא יהוה אֱלֹהִים אֶל־הָאָדָם וַיֹּאמֶר לוֹ אַיֶּכָה

(Va-yikra Adonai el ha-adam va-yomer lo ayekah)

"And the Lord, God, called Adam and said to him, where are you?"

[Genesis 3:9]

You, man, ask where the Almighty is? God turns back to you and says, "Where are you, O man? If you were to but live up to your responsibilities, you would not need to fear anything or anyone on this earth."

EYKHaH

LAMENTATIONS

We ask God how he could permit the major evils of history. The word we use, אֵיכָה (Eikhah), contains the four answers that remind us of our responsibilities.

א = 1 We dare not forget the requirement recited twice daily to "Hear O Israel, the Lord is our God, the Lord is One."

י = 10 The Lord whom we worship gave us Ten Commandments summarizing all of His law. It is to those ten principles that we made a commitment on Mount Sinai. Because we fail to heed them we deserve to be punished.

כ = 20 The age at which we are held accountable by divine law in the heavens above is 20. By then, we must be wise enough to understand the implications of the "One" and the ten, as well as the number five, which follows.

ה = 5 Five are the Books of Moses, every word of which we must treasure.

The "how" addressed to God finds its answer in the responsibilities transmitted to us in one, ten, twenty, and five.

BeKHY

WEEPING

On the Ninth of Av, we shed tears. We weep just as the prophet Jeremiah tells us the city of Jerusalem "truly weeps in the night, and her tears are on her cheeks" [Lamentations 1:2].

It is our weeping that will ensure that God has mercy upon us and turns our sorrow onto gladness. As the *Zohar*, the classic text of Jewish mysticism, teaches us: "There is no gate that tears cannot break through" [*Zohar*, Exodus 12b].

What is the power of בְּכִי (BeKHY), weeping? Its *gematria* is 32: ב = 2, כ = 20, י = 10 = 32. That is the numerical equivalent of the word לֵב (LeV), heart (ל = 30, ב = 2). Words that come from the heart are the ones most acceptable to the Almighty. Weeping has its source not from the lips, but from the depths of our souls.

Chapter 10
יוֹם הָעַצְמָאוּת
Israel Independence Day

כָּל הַמִּתְאַבֵּל עַל יְרוּשָׁלַיִם
זוֹכֶה וְרוֹאֶה בְּשִׂמְחָתָהּ

(Kol ha-mitabel al Yerushalayim zokheh ve-ro'eh be-simhatah)

תַּעֲנִית ל

Whoever mourns for Jerusalem
will merit to see it in its time of rejoicing

Taanit 30b

He IYYaR

THE FIFTH OF IYYAR

Two dates define the two most significant moments of our past, at the very beginning of our people's history.

On the fifteenth of נִיסָן (Nissan), we were redeemed from Egypt. That day is commemorated as the holiday of Passover. The letters that express this number corresponding to the birth of the Jewish nation are י-ה (י = 10, ה = 5). י-ה is not only the number 15, but the shortened form of the four-letter name of God, as in the oft-repeated prayer הַלְלוּיָה (Halleluyah)—praised be the Lord.

Passover is linked to שָׁבוּעוֹת (Shavu'ot). Freedom from Egypt is incomplete without freedom to be what we were intended to be, servants of the Lord who accept and live up to His Torah. Revelation took place on the sixth of סִיוָן (Sivan). That is the date of the holiday of שָׁבוּעוֹת (Shavu'ot). Six is identified by the letter ו—the very same letter that follows the י-ה in God's holy name of the Tetragrammaton.

Jewish history remained incomplete as long as the Jews remained in exile. Only in contemporary times did we finally realize our goal of returning to a national homeland and witnessing the reestablishment of the State of Israel. The date of this miraculous event, now celebrated as יוֹם הָעַצְמָאוּת (Yom Ha-Azma'ut), is the fifth of אִייָר (Iyyar). Five in Hebrew is the letter ה.

At long last, God's name has become completed through the very dates that best define His major appearances:

י-ה — the fifteenth of נִיסָן (Nissan): פֶּסַח (Pesaḥ)
ו — the sixth of סִיוָן (Sivan): שָׁבוּעוֹת (Shavu'ot)
ה — the fifth of אִייָר (Iyyar): יוֹם הָעַצְמָאוּת (Yom Ha-Azma'ut)

He IYYaR

THE FIFTH OF IYYAR

Why was the miracle of redemption in modern times divinely ordained to take place on the fifth day of אִיָּיר (Iyyar)?

The number five has special significance in Jewish thought. It is at the סֶדֶר (seder) meal on Passover that we outline the special meaning of every number:

Who knows one? I know one. One is our God in the Heavens and on earth.

Who knows two? I know two. Two are the tablets of the law.

Who knows three? I know three. Three are our forefathers—Abraham, Isaac, and Jacob.

Who knows four? I know four. Four are our mothers—Sarah, Rebecca, Rachel, and Leah.

Who knows five? I know five. Five are the books of the Torah.

We merit return to the land by virtue of our commitment to the word of the Lord. Israel and Torah are inseparable. That is why the date of יוֹם הָעַצְמָאוּת (Yom Ha-Aẓma'ut) alludes to the reason behind its prophetic fulfillment.

He IYYaR

THE FIFTH OF IYYAR

What is so special about the month of אִיָּיר (Iyyar) that makes it worthy to merit the modern day miracles of both יוֹם הָעַצְמָאוּת (Yom Ha-Aẓma'ut) as well as יוֹם יְרוּשָׁלַיִם (Yom Yerushalayim)?

Why was אִיָּיר (Iyyar) so unique to be doubly blessed with the contemporary moments of messianic fulfillment?

אִיָּיר (Iyyar) is an acronym. It is the month that contains within it the special merit of the three fathers—אַבְרָהָם (Avraham), יִצְחָק (Yizhak), and יַעֲקֹב (Ya'akov)—Abraham, Isaac, and Jacob. Their first letters, א, י, and י, give us the first three letters of the month. It is to each one of them that God vouchsafed the Holy Land. One other biblical figure towers above all others in terms of a link with the Holy Land. It is mother Rachel, רָחֵל (Raḥel), whom the prophet Jeremiah describes as רָחֵל מְבַכָּה עַל־בָּנֶיהָ (Raḥel mevakah al baneha), "Rachel weeping for her children" [Jeremiah 31:14]. It is to Rachel that God spoke with a promise: "Refrain your voice from weeping and your eyes from tears; for your works shall be rewarded, says the Lord, and they shall come back from the land of the enemy. There is hope for your future, says the Lord; and your children shall return to their own country" [Jeremiah 31:15–16].

The miracles of Israel today belong in the month of אִיָּיר (Iyyar)—acronym for the fathers to whom the land was promised and the mother whose tears insured that her descendants would be remembered.

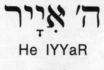

He IYYaR

THE FIFTH OF IYYAR

The word for five in Hebrew is חֲמִשָּׁה (ḥamishah).

It reminds us of the Five Books of Moses. But rearrange the letters and understand in a more profound way why this date was chosen for the return of our people to the Holy Land and the beginning of the process of messianic redemption. חֲמִשָּׁה (ḥamishah) contains the same letters as the word שִׂמְחָה (simḥah), joy and happiness.

Without a land, the Jews of dispersion were easy prey for the nations of the world. With Israel we regained a vital key to our national identity. When the Jews returned from their first captivity in Babylonia to the land of their fathers, they exclaimed: "הָיִינוּ שְׂמֵחִים (hayinu semeḥim)—we became those who rejoiced" [Psalm 126:3].

We, too, in modern times allow ourselves שִׂמְחָה (simḥah) because of what we were privileged to witness in the year 5708/1948, on the fifth day of the month of אִיָּר (Iyyar)—the חֲמִשָּׁה (ḥamishah), which represents our fulfillment of שִׂמְחָה (simḥah).

צִיּוֹן

ZiYON

❦

ZION

The prophet Isaiah had long ago foretold the fulfillment of the Zionist dream:

צִיּוֹן בְּמִשְׁפָּט תִּפָּדֶה וְשָׁבֶיהָ בִּצְדָקָה

(Ziyon be-mishpat tipadeh ve-shaveha be-zedakah)

"Zion shall be redeemed with justice and they that return of her with righteousness."

[Isaiah 1:27]

Messiah has not yet arrived even in the aftermath of the return of our people to Zion.

Jewish tradition speaks of two stages in the drama of Messianic fulfillment. The first is מָשִׁיחַ בֶּן יוֹסֵף (mashi'ah ben Yosef)—Messiah, son of Joseph. The second and final deliverer is מָשִׁיחַ בֶּן דָוִד (mashi'ah ben David)—Messiah, descendant of David.

What is the meaning of the strange precursor to the redeemer identified with David? יוֹסֵף (Yosef) in *gematria* is 156—י = 10, ו = 6, ס = 60, פ = 80 = 156. Joseph made it possible for the bones, עַצְמָאוֹת (azma'ot) of his father, Jacob, to find final resting place in the holy ground of Israel. As prime minister, he was able to accomplish politically the first return of an exiled Jew, Israel in very name, to the site for which he so urgently longed. צִיּוֹן (ZiYON), Zion, shares the same *gematria* (צ = 90, י = 10, ו = 6, נ = 50 = 156).

Zion today is the first step of the messianic dream. What יוֹסֵף (Yosef) did for the עַצְמָאוֹת (azma'ot) of his father, Israel, is represented today by צִיּוֹן (Ziyon), Zion, which from the יוֹם הָעַצְמָאוּת (Yom Ha-Azma'ut) of its inception allows the return of the people of Israel to its borders.

ZiYON

ZION

Why has it taken so long for the Jewish people to return to Zion?

What is it that made the land of our forefathers inaccessible to us throughout the centuries?

The holiness of צִיּוֹן (Ziyon), Zion, brought in its wake an unfortunate corollary. צִיּוֹן (Ziyon) in *gematria* is 156 (צ = 90, י = 10, ו = 6, ן = 50 = 156).

That is exactly the same *gematria* as the word קִנְאָה (KiNAH), jealousy, envy (ק = 100, נ = 50, א = 1, ה = 5 = 156).

צִיּוֹן (Ziyon) and קִנְאָה (kinah) are related for the simplest of truths. Francis Beaumont put it beautifully: "Envy, like the worm, never runs but to the fairest fruit; like a cunning bloodhound it singles out the fattest deer in the flock. Abraham's riches were the Philistines' envy, and Jacob's blessings had Esau's hatred."

The very proof of Zion's superior status is the numerical link between צִיּוֹן (Ziyon) and קִנְאָה (kinah).

צִיּוֹן

ZiYON

❦

ZION

צִיּוֹן (Ziyon), Zion, is a dream not only for a land, but of a mission.

Note carefully the last three letters of the word צִיּוֹן (Ziyon). They are readily recognizable to us as the name of a country and a culture that left an indelible stamp upon human history. יָוָן (Yavan) is Greece. The Greeks interacted with the Jews in the time of the battle between the Maccabees and the Hellenists. חֲנוּכָּה (Ḥanukkah), the holiday created out of this confrontation, represents the victory of the Judaic ideal over the Hellenic. The Greeks proclaimed "the holiness of beauty"; we insisted that far more significant is "the beauty of holiness."

But the ideal of beauty so emphatically stressed by the Greeks was not meant to be eliminated. Beauty deserves a place of honor when it is harnessed in the service of the good and the holy.

זֶה אֵלִי וְאַנְוֵהוּ
(Zeh eli ve-anvehu)

"This is my God and I will glorify Him."
[Exodus 15:2]

The letter denoting righteousness is the צ. Place the צ before the word יָוָן (Yavan) and you have צִיּוֹן (Ziyon), Zion. The glory of Greece remains if the first priority is the principle of righteousness. צִיּוֹן (Ziyon) is nothing other than holiness wedded to beauty—in the proper sequence.

Chapter 11
יוֹם יְרוּשָׁלַיִם
Jerusalem Reunification Day

אִם־אֶשְׁכָּחֵךְ יְרוּשָׁלָם
תִּשְׁכַּח יְמִינִי

(Im eshkaḥekh Yerushalayim tishkaḥ yemini)

תְּהִלִּים קלז:ה

If I forget you, O Jerusalem,
may my right hand forget its cunning.

Psalm 137:5

כ״ח אִיָיר

KHoF HeT IYYaR

TWENTY-EIGHTH DAY
OF IYYAR

יוֹם יְרוּשָׁלַיִם (Yom Yerushalayim) is on the twenty-eighth day of the month of אִיָיר (Iyyar). Twenty-eight in letters is כ״ח—two letters that make the word כֹּחַ (ko'aḥ), strength or power.

Elie Wiesel, the scribe of the Holocaust, movingly described the uniqueness of our generation: "We are the most cursed of all generations, and we are the most blessed of all generations. We are the generation of Job, but we are also the generation of Jerusalem."

The final solution as envisioned by our enemies was genocide. The final solution as predicted by our prophets was Jerusalem.

The Holocaust represented the weakness of the Jew. We were like sheep led to slaughter. Returning to our homeland gave us dignity. That is the meaning of יוֹם הָעַצְמָאוּת (Yom Ha-Aẓma'ut), marking the reestablishment of the State of Israel. The liberation of Jerusalem, spiritual center of the land of our fathers, returned to us the ultimate strength of our people.

קוֹל יהוה בַּכֹּחַ
(Kol Adonai ba-ko-aḥ)

"The voice of the Lord comes in strength."
[Psalm 29:4]

On the twenty-eighth day of אִיָיר (Iyyar), the day of כֹּחַ (ko'aḥ), we acknowledged God's strength in fulfilling His prophecies, even as we recognized the gift of return of the spiritual strength of our people through Jerusalem.

כ"ח אִיָּיר

KHoF ḤeT IYYaR

TWENTY-EIGHTH DAY OF IYYAR

There is one sin so common among the sons of man that the prophet constantly inveighed against it. Moses was concerned with it in his last speech to the people before his passing.

In his final oration, recorded in the Book of Deuteronomy, the Jewish leader warns lest "your heart be lifted up and you forget the Lord, your God, who brought you out of the land of Egypt, out of the house of bondage . . . and you say in your heart: 'My power and the might of my hand have gotten me this wealth' " [Deuteronomy 8:14–17].

Never ought mankind confuse blessings from the Almighty with personal achievement. "But you shall remember the Lord, your God, for it is He that gives you power to get wealth—כִּי הוּא הַנֹּתֵן לְךָ כֹּחַ (ki hu ha-noten lekha ko'aḥ)—It is He and He alone who gives unto you כֹּחַ, strength" [Deuteronomy 8:18].

כֹּחַ (ko'aḥ) comes from God alone. Could Jerusalem have been liberated on any day other than the twenty-eighth of אִיָּיר (Iyyar), the day of כֹּ"ח (ko'aḥ)?

It is the date itself that proclaims beyond question that:

זֶה-הַיּוֹם עָשָׂה יהוה נָגִילָה וְנִשְׂמְחָה בוֹ
(Zeh ha-yom asah Adonai nagilah ve-nismiḥah vo)

"This is the day that the Lord has made; we will rejoice and be glad on it."

[Psalm 118:24]

KHoF ḤeT IYYaR

TWENTY-EIGHTH DAY
OF IYYAR

The ultimate purpose of Jerusalem is powerfully portrayed by King David in the Book of Psalms:

יְרוּשָׁלַם הַבְּנוּיָה כְּעִיר שֶׁחֻבְּרָה־לָּהּ יַחְדָּו

(Yerushalayim ha-benuyah ke-ir she-ḥubrah lah yaḥdav)

"Jerusalem that is rebuilt is like a city that attaches to it together."

[Psalm 122:3]

Its function is to create unity between all Jews. Its goal is the word יַחְדָּו (yaḥdav)—the kind of togetherness manifested at Mount Sinai when

וַיַּעֲנוּ כָל־הָעָם יַחְדָּו וַיֹּאמְרוּ כֹּל אֲשֶׁר־דִּבֶּר יהוה נַעֲשֶׂה

(Va-ya'anu khol ha-am yaḥdav va-yomeru kol asher diber Adonai na-aseh)

"And all the people answered together and said 'All that the Lord has spoken, we will do.' "

[Exodus 19:8]

יַחְדָּו (YaḤDaV) in *gematria* is 28 (י = 10, ח = 8, ד = 4, ו = 6 = 28).

Jerusalem, the city of unity, the "twenty-eight" of יַחְדָּו (yaḥdav), was liberated on the twenty-eighth of אִיָּיר (Iyyar). After all, is not יַחְדָּו (yaḥdav), Jews being as one, the ultimate כֹּחַ (ko'aḥ) (28), power, of our people?

יְרוּשָׁלַיִם

YeRUSHaLaYiM

JERUSALEM

A Jew is commanded by God to be an optimist.

Despair bespeaks a lack of faith. Hopelessness is the antithesis of the religious personality.

The Talmud teaches us that in the World-to-Come we will be asked a series of questions. There is a final accounting after death to determine whether during our lifetimes we obeyed the most important dictates of the Almighty.

First and foremost, God will question us: צָפִיתָ לִישׁוּעָה? (ẓipita lishuah)—Did you await redemption? [*Shabbat* 31a]

הַתִּקְוָה (Ha-Tikvah), the hope, is not only the name of Israel's national anthem. It is the cardinal concept by which we must lead our lives, both personally and collectively.

Throughout the generations we never ceased saying לְשָׁנָה הַבָּאָה בִּירוּשָׁלַיִם (La-shanah ha-ba'ah bi-Yerushalayim)—Next year in Jerusalem. We close the סֵדֶר (seder), on Passover with that prayer even as we bring to an end the holy day of יוֹם כִּפּוּר (Yom Kippur) with these self-same words. No matter how much reality made the dream appear to be an impossibility, we never lost hope.

We took as divine imperative the words צַפֵּה לִישׁוּעָה (ẓapeh lishuah)—await redemption. The *gematria* of these words adds up to 596 (צ = 90, פ = 80, ה = 5; ל = 30, י = 10, שׁ = 300, ו = 6, ע = 70, ה = 5 = 596). The hope was finally fulfilled with the return to Jerusalem. How appropriate that the *gematria* of יְרוּשָׁלַיִם (YeRUSHaLaYiM), Jerusalem, is precisely the same, 596 (י = 10, ר = 200, ו = 6, שׁ = 300, ל = 30, י = 10, מ = 40 = 596).

יוֹם יְרוּשָׁלַיִם

YOM YeRUSHaLaYiM

JERUSALEM DAY

Before the miraculous events of the Six Day War, Jews were forbidden by the occupiers of Jerusalem to pray at their holiest site.

The Temple of old was built on Mount Moriah. That spot had previously been sanctified by the first Jew, Abraham, as he brought Isaac up as an offering on that very mountain to express his unqualified commitment to the commandments of God. That very spot, too, is where Adam had brought the first sacrifice ever offered by a human being to his Creator.

Tradition has it that the very mountain that served as the location for the first two Temples will have built upon it the Third and final Temple as well. It is called הַר הַבַּיִת (Har Ha-Bayit)—the mount of the house. הַר הַבַּיִת (HaR Ha-BaYiT) in *gematria* is 652 (ה = 5, ר = 200; ה = 5, ב = 2, י = 10, ת = 400 = 652). הַר הַבַּיִת (Har Ha-Bayit) was returned to us in modern times on יוֹם יְרוּשָׁלַיִם (Yom Yerushalayim). Can it be mere coincidence that the *gematria* of יוֹם יְרוּשָׁלַיִם (YOM YeRUSHaLaYiM) as well is 652 (י = 10, ו = 6, מ = 40; י = 10, ר = 200, ו = 6, ש = 300, ל = 30, י = 10, מ = 40 = 652).

Part II
Happy Days

Chapter 12
לֵידָה
Birth

אֵין רוּחַ הַקּוֹדֶשׁ
שׁוֹרֶה אֶלָּא עַל לֵב שְׂמֵחָה

(Ein ruaḥ ha-kodesh shoreh ela al lev semeḥah)

סֻכָּה ה:א

The Divine Spirit
rests only on a happy heart.

Sukkah 5:1

LeYDaH

BIRTH

The most precious gift God ever gave to the Jewish people was the gift of the Torah.

As the Jews departed from Egypt, God informed them that they would soon be granted this precious legacy. Anticipation of the event made it all the more memorable. They had to wait and to count the days from the Exodus to Revelation.

Forty-nine is the number of days that we count to recall the happiest day of our national history. The *gematria* of the word for birth, לֵידָה (LeYDaH), is also 49 (ל = 30, י = 10, ד = 4, ה = 5 = 49). Every birth is a renewed opportunity to add another recipient to those who received the message from God and to live in accordance with His teachings.

לֵידָה

LeYDaH

❧

BIRTH

Birth is a great blessing—no matter what the sex of the child. Before, there were but two, husband and wife. With לֵידָה (LeYDaH), birth, whose *gematria* is 49 (ל = 30, י = 10, ד = 4, ה = 5 = 49), there is now an addition to the family. The word that applies to the parents is וְגַם (ve-gam)—"and also." The *gematria* of וְגַם (Ve-GaM) is, of course, 49 (ו = 6, ג = 3, מ = 40 = 49).

Look at the letters of לֵידָה (leidah) and see that they are equally applicable to a son or a daughter. Rearrange them in one way and you have the word הַיֶּלֶד (ha-yeled)—the boy. Place the letters in a different order and you have the word יַלְדָה (yaldah)—a girl.

No matter which one, the response of parent must be the grateful acknowledgment that זֶה הָיָה טוֹב (ZeH HaYaH TOV)—this was good. The *gematria* of this phrase, too, is 49, corresponding to לֵידָה (leidah) or הַיֶּלֶד (ha-yeled) or יַלְדָה (yaldah) (ז = 7, ה = 5; ה = 5, י = 10, ה = 5; ט = 9, ו = 6, ב = 2 = 49).

מַזָּל טוֹב

MaZaL TOV

MAZEL TOV

A joyous occasion brings forth congratulations of מַזָּל טוֹב (mazal tov).

מַזָּל (mazal) refers to the constellations. On a simple level, it expresses the hope that the stars be aligned in a proper manner so that good fortune follow.

We know, however, that true מַזָּל (mazal) is nothing other than divine destiny; good fortune is the finger of God indelibly inscribing the handwriting on the wall for our future. מַזָּל (mazal) is God "being gracious unto us."

As a biblical blessing, we find the idea beautifully conveyed in בִּרְכַּת כֹּהֲנִים (Birkat Kohanim), the Priestly Benediction:

יָאֵר יהוה פָּנָיו אֵלֶיךָ וִיחֻנֶּךָּ
(Ya'er Adonai panav eleikha vi-huneka)

"The Lord make His Face to shine upon you and be gracious unto you."

[Numbers 6:25]

The *gematria* of וִיחֻנֶּךָּ (ViY-HuNeKa) is 94 (ו = 6, י = 10, ח = 8, נ = 50, כ = 20 = 94).

Ninety-four is the *gematria* as well of the words מַזָּל טוֹב (MaZaL TOV) (מ = 40, ז = 7, ל = 30; ט = 9, ו = 6, ב = 2 = 94). May your good fortune be that God Himself be gracious unto you.

מַזָּל טוֹב

MaZaL TOV

MAZEL TOV

There are two kinds of happy moments for which Jewish law requires a blessing of thanksgiving.

When a joyous event occurs that brings happiness only to the individual directly involved, the blessing to be recited is שֶׁהֶחֱיָנוּ וְקִיְּמָנוּ וְהִגִּיעָנוּ לַזְּמַן הַזֶּה (she-heḥeyanu ve-kiyemanu ve-higiyanu la-z'man ha-zeh). We are to thank God for keeping us alive and allowing us to reach this moment of joy.

If, however, the blessing for which we give thanks is one that in its beneficence affects others for good as well, the text of the בְּרָכָה (berakhah) differs. Jewish law demands not שֶׁהֶחֱיָנוּ (she-heḥeyanu), but rather the words הַטּוֹב וְהַמֵּטִיב (ha-tov ve-ha-metiv). We thank God "who does good and causes good unto others."

The *gematria* of הַטּוֹב וְהַמֵּטִיב (Ha-TOV Ve-Ha-MeTiYV) is 94 (ה = 5, ט = 9, ו = 6, ב = 2; ו = 6, ה = 5, מ = 40, ט = 9, י = 10, ב = 2 = 94). That is the *gematria* of מַזָּל טוֹב (MaZaL TOV) (מ = 40, ז = 7, ל = 30; ט = 9, ו = 6, ב = 2 = 94). A מַזָּל טוֹב (mazal tov) is offered for the higher moments of joy when rejoicing is not restricted to one person, but is shared by the many.

מַזָּל

MaZaL

FORTUNE/LUCK

Luck doesn't just happen. We are not the products of haphazard events; our lives do not reflect the results of happenstance or coincidence. What is מַזָּל (mazal)? It is an acronym for the three things that determine our fates and our destinies:

מ is the first letter of the word מָקוֹם (makom), place. First and foremost, we must be in the right place.

ז is the first letter of the word זְמַן (zeman), time. We must know the right moment.

ל is the first letter of the word לִמוּד (limud), study or learning.

The right place, the right time, and the wisdom to know how to make the most of them lead to what those who are simple will describe as nothing other than מַזָּל (mazal).

YeLeD

❦

A BOY

In days of old, a child was considered a blessing because there was "another hand."

A boy could assist in the fields. He could work with his father. When there were no machines to assist in physical labor, the value of an added hand could not be lightly esteemed.

In Hebrew the word יַד (yad), hand, does appear in the word יֶלֶד (yeled). It is an aspect of the child, but it is not central to our understanding of his worth. In the very middle of the word for a child is the ל (lamed). That letter stands for learning, for study.

The most important reason to rejoice with a יֶלֶד (yeled) is that there is now another human being on earth, created in God's image, who can learn the will of his Creator and thereby fulfill the most important מִצְוָה (mizvah) of our faith:

וְתַלְמוּד תּוֹרָה כְּנֶגֶד כּוּלָם
(Ve-talmud torah ke-neged kulam)

"And the study of Torah stands above all else."

[*Shabbat* 127a]

YaLDaH

A GIRL

Women by nature are more spiritual than men. The *Midrash* says that is why when God was preparing to give the Torah on Mount Sinai to the Jewish people, he instructed Moses first to call to the women and then to the men:

כֹּה תֹאמַר לְבֵית יַעֲקֹב וְתַגֵּיד לִבְנֵי יִשְׂרָאֵל
(Koh tomar le-veit Ya'akov ve-tageid le-v'nei Yisrael)

"Thus shall you say to the house of Jacob (the women) and tell the children of Israel (the men)."
[Exodus 19:3]

Indeed, Jewish law will rule that religious descent is matrilineal. If the mother is Jewish, then so is the child. It is her status alone that determines the religious definition of the next generation.

יַלְדָּה (yaldah) is surrounded on its two sides by the letters י and ה. Join them together and they form the word יָה (Yah). That is the short form of the four-letter name of God. If you are blessed with a girl, then הַלְלוּיָהּ (Halleluyah)—praise the Lord who gave you part of Himself in feminine form.

YaLDaH

A GIRL

A daughter is a special blessing for a father.

It is within the nature of things for sons to have a greater feeling for their mothers. But daughters love their fathers in a way that defies explanation.

יַלְדָה (YaLDaH) in *gematria* is 49 (י = 10, ל = 30, ד = 4, ה = 5 = 49). That is the *gematria* of בְּאַהֲבָה לְאַבָּא (Be-AHaVaH Le-ABA)—with love for father (ב = 2, א = 1, ה = 5, ב = 2, ה = 5; ל = 30; א = 1, ב = 2, א = 1 = 49).

Chapter 13
בְּרִית מִילָה
Circumcision

זֹאת בְּרִיתִי אֲשֶׁת תִּשְׁמְרוּ בֵּינִי

וּבֵינֵיכֶם וּבֵין זַרְעֲךָ אַחֲרֶיךָ

הִמּוֹל לָכֶם כָּל־זָכָר

(Zot beriti asher tishmeru beini u-veineikhem u-vein
zarakha aḥarekha himol lakhem kol zakhar)

בְּרֵאשִׁית טז:י

This is my covenant
that you shall keep
between Me and you
and your descendants after you;
every male among you shall be circumcised.

Genesis 17:10

הַמֵּפֵר בְּרִיתוֹ שֶׁל אַבְרָהָם

אָבִינוּ . . . אֵין לוֹ חֵלֶק

לְעוֹלָם הַבָּא

(Ha-mefer brito shel Avraham Avinu . . . ein lo ḥelek
la-olam ha-ba)

אָבוֹת ג:טו

He who nullifies the covenant
of our forefather, Abraham . . .
has no share in the World to Come.

Ethics of the Fathers 3:15

בְּרִית
BRiYT

COVENANT/CIRCUMCISION

In the song the Jews sang when they safely crossed the Red Sea, they exclaimed:

זֶה אֵלִי וְאַנְוֵהוּ
(Zeh Eli ve-anvehu)

"This is my God and I will glorify Him."
[Exodus 15:2]

The Talmud [*Shabbat* 133b] sees in the word וְאַנְוֵהוּ (ve-anvehu) a more profound meaning: וְאַנְוֵהוּ (ve-anvehu)—הֱוֵי דוֹמֶה לוֹ (havei domeh lo)—"be comparable unto Him." We read the word as a construct of two shorter words: אֲנִי (ani), I, and הוּא (hu), He. We must strive to be like the Creator. Every divine trait serves as inspiration for us to be imitated.

To be a Jew is to model our lives after Him. The covenant that proclaims our commitment is בְּרִית (brit). The *gematria* of בְּרִית (BRiYT) is 612 (ב = 2, ר = 200, י = 10, ת = 400 = 612). Although there are 613 commandments, not just 612, one of those 613 is "I am the Lord, your God, who took you out of the land of Egypt, the house of bondage." While counted as a מִצְוָה (mizvah), the existence of God is a reality—whether we believe in Him or not. The first of the Ten Commandments asks us to acknowledge the creator but is also independently demonstrated by creation itself. At the very moment of birth, "I am the Lord, your God . . ." is made manifest. What remains for the eighth day is to commit to 612 laws, whose purpose is to imitate Him in all of our ways.

The commitment we assume with the covenant on the eighth day is to be *like* God—not to be God. We believe in the Almighty and we accept upon ourselves with בְּרִית (BRiYT) (612), the requirement to imitate Him in all of His ways.

בְּרִית

BRiYT

COVENANT/CIRCUMCISION

The very first word in the Torah is בְּרֵאשִׁית (bereshit), in the beginning.

The very first מִצְוָה (miẓvah) for a Jewish boy is that of בְּרִית (berit). So important is this covenant that we are taught:

חֲבִיבָה הַמִּילָה שֶׁנִּשְׁבַּע הַקָּדוֹשׁ בָּרוּךְ הוּא לְאַבְרָהָם שֶׁכָּל מִי שֶׁהוּא מָהוּל אֵינוֹ יוֹרֵד לְגֵיהִנּוֹם

(Havivah ha-milah she-nishba ha-kadosh Barukh Hu le-Avraham she-kol mi she-hu mahul eino yored le-Gehinom)

"Precious is circumcision, for the Almighty swore to Abraham that whoever is circumcised will not descend to Gehinnom."

[*Tanḥuma, Lekh Lekha*, 20]

Hidden in the opening word of the Torah, בְּרֵאשִׁית (bereshit), are two smaller words: בְּרִית (berit), covenant, and אֵשׁ (esh), fire. The first priority is to stamp our seed with the covenant of Abraham, to spare them the fires of גֵיהִנּוֹם (Gehinom) in the afterworld.

MiYLaH

CIRCUMCISION

On the biblical phrase, בְּצֶלֶם אֱלֹהִים בָּרָא אֹתוֹ (be-ẓelem Elohim bara oto), "in the image of God He created him" [Genesis 1:27], the *Targum* comments that God gave him the "spirit of speech."

What makes mankind different than the animal kingdom? In Jewish thought, our uniqueness resides in the power of speech. With our mouths we can utter prayers to God, study the holy words of Torah, and communicate truths to our fellow man. We share our bodies with the animal world. It is our mouths that make us human; it is the use of our tongues that allows us to become almost divine.

מִילָה (milah), circumcision, defines Jewish males as Jews. מִילָה (MiYLaH) in *gematria* is 85 (מ = 40, י = 10, ל = 30, ה = 5 = 85). That is the *gematria* of פֶּה (PeH), mouth (פ = 80, ה = 5 = 85).

With the words of our mouths we will fulfill the covenant.

מִילָה

MiYLaH

CIRCUMCISION

How dare we alter that which God has made? A child is born uncircumcised. Surely that must be God's will. Should that which God created not be left exactly so?

When the Roman emperor asked Rabbi Akiva precisely this question, the response of the great sage conveyed a fundamental teaching of Jewish thought. God did not create a perfect world. He purposely left it incomplete so that man might play a role in ongoing creation. Doctors can heal, scientists may discover, the very face of the earth may be altered to improve the conditions of man. God created in seven days and on the eighth He said to man, "Now you take over and continue what I have begun."

מִילָה (milah), circumcision, takes place on the eighth day for that reason. Man alters and improves upon what God has created, for man's role, as the Jerusalem Talmud puts it, is to be שׁוּתָף עִם הַקָּדוֹשׁ בָּרוּךְ הוּא בְּמַעֲשֵׂה בְּרֵאשִׁית (Shutaf im Ha-Kodosh Barukh Hu be-ma'aseh bereshit)—a partner with God in the act of creation.

מִילָה (MiYLaH) in *gematria* is 85 (מ = 40, י = 10, ל = 30, ה = 5 = 85). Its purpose is to make man כָּמֹכָה (kamokhah), like You, the Creator. כָּמֹכָה (KaMoKHaH) in *gematria* is also 85 (כ = 20, מ = 40, כ = 20, ה = 5 = 85).

מִילָה

MiYLaH

CIRCUMCISION

At a circumcision, the hope is traditionally expressed that

כְּשֵׁם שֶׁנִּכְנַס לַבְּרִית, כֵּן יִכָּנֵס לְתוֹרָה וּלְחֻפָּה וּלְמַעֲשִׂים טוֹבִים
(Ke-shem she-nikhnas la-berit, ken yekanes le-Torah,
u-le-ḥuppah, u-le-ma'asim tovim)

"Just as the child entered the covenant of *berit*, so, too, may he enter to Torah, to *ḥuppah* (the marital canopy), and to good deeds."

[*Shabbat* 137b]

Why is circumcision the paradigm for all other good deeds? It is the one מִצְוָה (miẓvah) that is, by definition, everlasting. It is a stamp of identity upon the person that always remains and cannot be altered.

מִילָה (milah), circumcision, identifies one as a Jew forever. מִילָה (MiYLaH) in *gematria* is 85 (מ = 40, י = 10, ל = 30, ה = 5 = 85). With מִילָה (milah), the child becomes כְּאוּמָה זוּ (ke-umah zu)—like this nation. כְּאוּמָה זוּ (ke-umah zu) shares the same *gematria* as מִילָה (MiYLaH)—85 (כ = 20, א = 1, ו = 6, מ = 40, ה = 5; ז = 7, ו = 6 = 85).

שֵׁם

SHeM

NAME

At the circumcision, a Jewish boy is also given a name.

A name, in Jewish tradition, is more than a descriptive. It also represents one's destiny.

A divine spirit aids parents in deciding which name they should give to their child. A name is the script for an entire lifetime. כִּי־כִשְׁמוֹ כֵּן הוּא (ki khe-shemo ken hu), "as his name, so is he" [1 Samuel 25:25].

Every person's life is a סֵפֶר (sefer), a book. As the Torah says, זֶה סֵפֶר תּוֹלְדֹת אָדָם (zeh sefer toldot adam), "This is the book of the generations of Adam" [Genesis 5:1].

סֵפֶר (SeFeR), book, in *gematria* adds up to 340 (ס = 60, פ = 80, ר = 200 = 340). Name, שֵׁם (SHeM), too, is 340 (ש = 300, מ = 40 = 340). Our name is the most succinct summary of the סֵפֶר (sefer) of our lives.

Chapter 14

בַּר מִצְוָה/בַּת מִצְוָה
Bar Mitzvah/Bat Mitzvah

בִּנְעָרֵינוּ וּבִזְקֵנֵינוּ נֵלֵךְ
בְּבָנֵינוּ וּבִבְנוֹתֵנוּ

(Be-ne'areinu u-vizkeneinu nelekh be-vaneinu
u-vivnotenu)

שְׁמוֹת י:ט

We will go with our young and
with our old,
with our sons and with our daughters.

Exodus 10:9

בַּר מִצְוָה/בַּת מִצְוָה
BaR MiZVaH/BaT MiZVaH

BAR MITZVAH/
BAT MITZVAH

Twice a day, before retiring to bed at night and when arising in the morning, we recite the שְׁמַע יִשְׂרָאֵל (Shema Yisrael) prayer. It summarizes the most important commitments of our faith.

First and foremost, we proclaim our belief in monotheism: "Hear, O Israel, the Lord is our God, the Lord is One."

We follow that by defining our relationship with God as one based upon love—"You shall love the Lord, your God, with all your heart, and with all your soul, and with all of your might." These are words commanded to be "placed upon your heart." But that alone, of course, cannot suffice. A Judaism kept to oneself alone has no future. The key to our survival is contained in the phrase:

וְשִׁנַּנְתָּם לְבָנֶיךָ וְדִבַּרְתָּ בָּם
(Ve-shinantam le-vanekha ve-dibarta bam)

"And you shall teach them to your children, and you shall speak of them."

[Deuteronomy 6:7]

The word בָּם (bam), according to our sages, is an acronym for *what* shall be taught and transmitted:

ב is the first letter of the written law, the Torah—בְּרֵאשִׁית (bereshit).

מ is the first letter of the oral law, מֵאֵימָתַי קוֹרִין אֶת שְׁמַע (me'eimatai korin et shema), "From when do we read the *shema*?" which is the opening phrase of the first *mishnah* in the tractate of *Berakhot*.

The word כָּם (bam) is also an acronym for the age at which our children must assume personal responsibility. The letters of כָּם (bam) stand for בַּר מִצְוָה (bar miẓvah) or בַּת מִצְוָה (bat miẓvah). We must teach our children so that when they become of age, they can carry on in their lives what has been transmitted to us by our past.

בַּר מִצְוָה

BaR MiZVaH

BAR MITZVAH

The *Mishnah* in *Ethics of the Fathers* teaches us בֶּן שְׁלֹשׁ עֶשְׂרֵה לַמִּצְוֹת (ben shelosh esreih la-miẓvot), "at thirteen years old becomes obliged to observe the commandments" [Ethics of the Fathers 5:25].

Thirteen is a number with special significance. It represents the *gematria* of the word אַהֲבָה (AHaVaH)—love (א $= 1$, ה $= 5$, ב $= 2$, ה $= 5 = 13$).

At thirteen, the actions of a young lad are no longer imitative of parent or the result of fear of one's forebears. At thirteen, one can make a conscious, voluntary personal commitment. It is then that a young boy may be said to truly "love the Lord, his God." God then returns love in equal measure. It is love from below and love from above—the thirteen of man's אַהֲבָה (ahavah) merged with the thirteen of the Almighty's—that merge to make the number 26. That is the *gematria* of God's holy four-letter name, יהוה (י $= 10$, ה $= 5$, ו $= 6$, ה $= 5 = 26$).

When man and God meet in mutual love, that is divinity in its highest form.

בַּר מִצְוָה

BaR MiZVaH

BAR MITZVAH

On the סֶדֶר (seder) night, Jews read a small prayer that expresses the deeper significance of the first thirteen numbers.

Every one of them has a story to tell. Every one of them is a reminder of an essential concept or category within our faith: One is our God; two are the tablets of the Decalogue; three are our forefathers, Abraham, Isaac, and Jacob; four are our matriarchs—Sarah, Rebecca, Rachel, and Leah; five are the books of the Torah; six are the books of the Mishnah; seven are the days of the Shabbat; eight are the days of circumcision; nine are the months of pregnancy; ten are the commandments; eleven are the stars in Joseph's dream; twelve are the tribes; and thirteen are God's attributes.

Every time that we mention a new number in this prayer, we revert back to the ones that preceded going all the way back to one. Everything has its source in that one—the One who created the heavens and the earth.

When a young lad reaches the age of thirteen and becomes Bar Mitzvah, his life must now be guided by the recognition of the One of the universe. One in Hebrew is אֶחָד (EHaD). In *gematria* that adds up to 13 (א = 1, ח = 8, ד = 4 = 13). It is at thirteen that we are wise enough to recognize and to acknowledge that everything in this world—our wealth, our talents, and our very being—all come from the אֶחָד (Eḥad), the One, whom we worship.

בַּר מִצְוָה

BaR MiẐVaH

BAR MITZVAH

A Bar Mitzvah boy has completed thirteen years of life on this earth. He celebrates on his birthday, which in fact is י"ג שָׁנִים וְיוֹם אֶחָד (Yud-gimmel shanim ve-yom eḥad), thirteen years and a day.

Now he starts the fourteenth year of his life.

Fourteen in Hebrew is י"ד. That is not only a number, but a word as well. It stands for יַד (yad), hand.

With entry into the year of יַד (yad), the young man is expected to act and to do, to stretch forth his hand and to accomplish, to be a productive member of society and of the Jewish people. Until now everything had been done for the child.

Maturity brings forth obligations. Intelligence demands action. If you are wise enough to know right from wrong, then Torah law demands that you practice with your hand what is now clear to you in your head.

בַּר מִצְוָה

BaR MiẒVaH

BAR MITZVAH

The total *gematria* of the two words בַּר מִצְוָה (BaR MiẒVaH) is 343 (ב = 2, ר = 200; מ = 40, צ = 90, ו = 6, ה = 5 = 343).

What is the most important message we can give to a young man as he reaches the age of maturity and manhood? It is לֵךְ בְּדֶרֶךְ טוֹבִים (lekh be-derekh tovim), go on the path of the good.

The numerical total of that phrase is also precisely 343 (ל = 30, ך = 20; ב = 2, ד = 4, ר = 200, כ = 20; ט = 9, ו = 6, ב = 2, י = 10, ם = 40 = 343). The name of the day and its hero—the בַּר מִצְוָה (bar miẓvah)—are numerically identical to the major message conveyed at this auspicious moment: Because you are now responsible for your actions, follow the way of the righteous all the rest of the days of your life.

בַּת מִצְוָה

BaT MiZVaH

BAT MITZVAH

Girls mature more rapidly than boys.

Boys must wait until the age of thirteen. Girls are considered capable of understanding—and thus of responsibility—a year before males, at the age of twelve.

בַּת מִצְוָה (BaT MiZVaH) in *gematria* is 543 (בּ = 2, ת = 400; מ = 40, צ = 90, ו = 6, ה = 5 = 543).

As young women, they are now welcomed בְּיִשְׂרָאֵל (be-Yisrael)—into the community of Israel. The *gematria* of בְּיִשְׂרָאֵל (Be-YiSRaEL) is the very same 543 (בּ = 2, י = 10, שׁ = 300, ר = 200, א = 1, ל = 30 = 543).

At age twelve a בַּת מִצְוָה (bat miẓvah) is בְּיִשְׂרָאֵל (be-Yisrael). As she fulfills her destiny to become a mother in Israel, she will also determine who is a Jew, for lineage in Jewish law is determined by the religion of the mother. From the age of twelve on, she will determine who is considered בְּיִשְׂרָאֵל (be-Yisrael), within the community of Israel.

Chapter 15

נְשׂוּאִין
Marriage

וַיֹּאמֶר יהוה אֱלֹהִים

לֹא־טוֹב הֱיוֹת הָאָדָם לְבַדּוֹ

אֶעֱשֶׂה־לּוֹ עֵזֶר כְּנֶגְדּוֹ

(Va-yomer Adonai Elohim lo tov heyot ha-adam levado;
eheh'seh lo ezer kenegdo)

בְּרֵשִׁית ב:יח

And the Lord, God, said:
It is not good that the man
should be alone;
I will make him a helpmeet for him.

Genesis 2:18

עַל־כֵּן יַעֲזָב־אִישׁ אֶת־אָבִיו

וְאֶת־אִמּוֹ וְדָבַק בְּאִשְׁתּוֹ

וְהָיוּ לְבָשָׂר אֶחָד

(Al ken ya'azov ish et aviv ve-et imo ve-davak be-ishto
ve-hayu le-vasar eḥad)

בְּרֵאשִׁית ב:כד

Therefore shall a man leave his father
and his mother
and shall cleave unto his wife
and they shall be one flesh.

Genesis 2:24

כַּלָּה

KaLaH

꧁꧂

BRIDE

The *Midrash* tells of a deeply religious couple who could not live together and eventually divorced. Each one remarried. The wife found a man who was not observant. In a short while after their marriage, their home reflected the piety that had been part of the woman's tradition throughout her lifetime. Her ex-husband, too, married someone who was not observant. His story, however, had a far different ending. His new wife drew him after her heretical values and viewpoints. The man who had loved his faith and his God had his heart turned by his new partner.

The midrashic tale is meant to teach a profound truth about human behavior. The religious definition of a home is most often determined by the woman of the household.

The bride is called כַּלָּה (kallah). כָּל (kol) all, ה, five, i.e., the Five Books of Moses and adherence to Torah are subsumed under her. Be very careful whom you take as bride because she will create the religious climate for the family.

כַּלָּה

KaLaH

❦

BRIDE

When Moses asked to see God, the divine response was וְרָאִיתָ אֶת־אֲחֹרָי (ve-ra'ita et aḥorai), "and you will see my back" [Exodus 33:23]. God, of course, has no physical form. It is one of the Thirteen Principles of Maimonides that the Almighty has neither bodily parts nor human appearance.

What God meant, according to biblical commentators, is that He will be perceived only in retrospect. It is often only after something has transpired that we can really grasp its true meaning.

So, too, is it at times with those who mean the most to our lives. The word הָלַךְ (halakh) means "He walked, he went, he took a certain direction." What makes someone walk on the path of his life? What is most responsible for the direction a man takes during the course of his lifetime? The answer most often is to look at the word הָלַךְ (halakh) in retrospect. Read the letters in reverse and they spell כַּלָּה (kallah), bride.

The woman a man marries is most responsible for the path of his days and the way in which he goes on this earth.

KaLaH

BRIDE

At the wedding ceremony, the bride marches around the groom seven times.

It is a symbolic reminder of a famous moment in Jewish history. Joshua marched around the city of Jericho seven times before he conquered it. So, too, has the bride conquered the heart of her husband.

A bride is טוֹב לִבּוֹ (tov libo)—the perfection of his heart. כַּלָה (KaLaH) in *gematria* is 55 (כ = 20, ל = 30, ה = 5 = 55) She is everything that is considered good in his heart—for the *gematria* of טוֹב לִבּוֹ (TOV LiBO) is also 55 (ט = 9, ו = 6 ב = 2; ל = 30, ב = 2, ו = 6 = 55).

כַּלָה

KaLaH

BRIDE

For everything from which we derive benefit there is a blessing to be recited.

We give thanks when we eat a fruit from the tree, a vegetable from the ground. We acknowledge the עֵץ (eẓ), the tree, and the אֲדָמָה (adamah), the ground, in these respective בְּרָכוֹת (berakhot).

There are a number of blessings that are quite specific. But there is one blessing that is almost all inclusive. Indeed, Jewish law decrees that when we are uncertain about which particular blessing to recite, the "all-inclusive blessing" may be used.

Its text is simple. We bless the Lord, King of the Universe, שֶׁהַכֹּל נִהְיֶה בִּדְבָרוֹ (she-hakol nihyeh be-devaro)—that everything is by His word.

הַכֹּל (ha-kol)—"everything"—comes from the Almighty. Rearrange the letters and know that כַּלָה (kallah), a bride, also comes from the Lord above. Forty days before birth a heavenly voice proclaims, "The daughter of So-and-So to So-and-So."

Man searches for a bride only to rediscover what God had originally ordained for him.

חָתָן

HaTaN

GROOM

Ask any Jewish parent what they most want from their children and they will tell you. The word is נַחַת (naḥas—Ashkenazic; naḥat—Sephardic). No English term can fully convey its meaning.

It is the joy brought about by living up to expectations. It is the happiness that comes from knowing that a child is all that he can be. It is being recompensed for all the travails of parenthood with the moments that make life meaningful and sacrifices worthwhile.

Because we understand the truth of the biblical passage that "it is not good for man to be alone," we pray at the very first שִׂמְחָה (simḥah) we celebrate with the child, at the circumcision, that

כְּשֵׁם שֶׁנִּכְנַס לַבְּרִית, כֵּן יִכָּנֵס לְתוֹרָה וּלְחֻפָּה וּלְמַעֲשִׂים טוֹבִים
(Ke-shem she-nikhnas la-berit, ken yekanes le-Torah,
u-le-ḥuppah, u-le-ma'asim tovim)

"Just as we were privileged to witness this child coming to the covenant of circumcision, so, too, may he enter to Torah, to marriage, and to good deeds."

[*Shabbat* 137b]

A boy is all of eight days old and already we make mention of the נַחַת (naḥat) we hope to see when he becomes a חָתָן (ḥatan). Not strange at all if we consider that the letters of נַחַת (naḥat) and חָתָן (ḥatan) are the same. There is no greater joy or moment of fulfillment than when the child we have brought into this world stands prepared to form his own household and begin anew the creation of yet another generation.

חָתָן

HaTaN

GROOM

Forty days before the creation of child, a heavenly voice goes forth and proclaims that So-and-So is destined for So-and-So [*Sotah* 2a].

Why does God arrange marriages before birth? Why not wait until boy and girl grow, mature, and develop physically so that their prospective union could be judged on the basis of what they look like in years more proximate to the actual wedding? Because, the sages explain, God brings together not bodies, but souls. It is the spiritual essence and the inner core of a man and a woman that precede even their birth that determines the suitability of one for another.

Who is a חָתָן (ḥatan)? In *gematria* חָתָן (ḤaTaN) is 458 (ח = 8, ת = 400, נ = 50 = 458). That is the *gematria* also of יְדִיד נֶפֶשׁ (YeDiYD NeFeSH) (י = 10, ד = 4, י = 10, ד = 4; נ = 50, פ = 80, שׁ = 300 = 458). יְדִיד נֶפֶשׁ (yedid nefesh) means beloved of soul. The groom is a soulmate for the bride. Man and woman must work at a marriage — but God has already proclaimed that these souls have the potential to be suitable for each other.

חָתָן

HaTaN

GROOM

Bachelors are sinners in the eyes of Jewish tradition.

Said Rabbi Elazar: "Every man who does not have a wife is not a man. As the Torah says: 'Male and female, He had created them and blessed them and called their name Adam' [Genesis 5:2]. Only when man is joined to woman does he deserve the designation אָדָם (Adam), human being" [*Yevamot* 63a].

That is why one of the seven blessings recited at a wedding gives thanks unto God, יוֹצֵר הָאָדָם (yoẓer ha-adam), who created a human being. Not at birth do we say these words, but we wait until the wedding. That is when a mother and father can finally rejoice because at last they have a child who has become fully human in choosing to merge with another and create a family.

יִשְׂמַח אָבִיךָ וְאִמֶּךָ (yismaḥ avikha ve-imekha)—"Your father and your mother will rejoice" in *gematria* adds up to 458 (י = 10, שׂ = 300, מ = 40, ח = 8; א = 1, ב = 2, י = 10, כ = 20; ו = 6, א = 1, מ = 40, כ = 20 = 458). The fulfillment of 458 is not at birth or even at בַּר מִצְוָה (bar miẓvah), but when a boy becomes a חָתָן (HaTaN), which in *gematria* is also 458 (ח = 8, ת = 400, נ = 50 = 458).

KaLaH/ḤaTaN

BRIDE/GROOM

After the creation of every day, God looked at what he had made and said, "Behold it is good." But after the creation of Adam, he added:

וַיֹּאמֶר יהוה אֱלֹהִים לֹא־טוֹב הֱיוֹת הָאָדָם לְבַדּוֹ אֶעֱשֶׂה־לּוֹ עֵזֶר כְּנֶגְדּוֹ
(Va-yomer Adonai Elohim lo tov heyot ha-adam levado
eh'ehseh lo ezer kenegdo)

"And the Lord, God, said: It is not good that the man should be alone; I will make him a helpmeet for him."

[Genesis 2:18]

Everything previously created would still not deserve the adjective טוֹב (tov), good, unless it could be experienced by a human being with another. Happiness consists only in seeing things through four eyes, not two.

One person means loneliness. Two people together represents the potential for joy and for achievement. As King Solomon put it, טוֹבִים הַשְּׁנַיִם מִן־הָאֶחָד (tovim ha-shenayim min ha-eḥad), "Two are better than one" [Ecclesiastes 4:9]. Man and woman together have the power to make each other happy, to bring new life into this world, to create a family and to build a home on the foundation of mutual love and respect.

Take the first letters of כַּלָּה (kallah) and חָתָן (ḥatan) and you have the word כֹּחַ (ko'aḥ), strength or power. Bride and groom brought together are the strength of our faith and our people.

---

190   HAPPY DAYS

KaLaH/ḤaTaN

BRIDE/GROOM

The prophet Zechariah gave us a powerful statement about the true source of success. He taught us that throughout the ages, success depends not on the strength of human endeavor, but rather upon the divine spirit:

לֹא בְחַיִל וְלֹא בְכֹחַ כִּי אִם־בְּרוּחִי אָמַר יהוה צְבָאוֹת
(Lo ve-ḥayil ve-lo ve-kho'aḥ ki im be-ru'ḥi amar
Adonai Zeva'ot)

"Not by might, nor by power, but by My Spirit, says the Lord of Hosts."

[Zechariah 4:6]

This, too, is the secret of every marriage. Upon whom does the success of the home ultimately rest? One might perhaps assume that it is the woman. After all, the ideal wife is referred to by King Solomon as אֵשֶׁת חַיִל (eshet ḥayil)—a woman of valor [Proverbs 31:10]. Says the prophet, לֹא בְחַיִל (lo ve-ḥayil), one cannot place prime responsibility for a successful marriage upon the wife alone, no matter how precious or worthy she may be. The prophet continues, וְלֹא בְכֹחַ (ve-lo ve-ko'aḥ). The word כֹּחַ (ko'aḥ) is acronym for כַּלָּה/חָתָן (kallah/ḥatan), bride/groom. Even husband and wife together do not make a home, achieve a successful marriage, or build a family without inviting the most important Partner to their union. כִּי אִם־בְּרוּחִי אָמַר יהוה צְבָאוֹת (ki im be-ru'ḥi amar Adonai Zeva'ot). But only with My Spirit, says the Lord of Hosts.

When the אֵשֶׁת חַיִל (eshet ḥayil), the woman of valor, together with the כֹּחַ (ko'aḥ) of כַּלָּה/חָתָן (kallah/ḥatan), bride/groom, add the spirit of God, then their union will be blessed.

כַּלָה/חָתָן
KaLaH/ḤaTaN

BRIDE/GROOM

Marriage takes place under a חֻפָּה (ḥuppah), a canopy. It is a symbol of the heavens above. Bride and groom stand together ready to be wed because it was decreed from the heavens that they come together on this day.

In *gematria* חָתָן (ḤaTaN) and כַּלָה (KaLaH) together add up to 513. חָתָן = 458: ח = 8, ת = 400, נ = 50; כַּלָה = 55: כ = 20, ל = 30, ה = 5. 55 + 458 = 513.

Their merger is divinely decreed: וְזִוּוּג מִן הַשָּׁמַיִם (Ve-ZiVUG MiN Ha-SHaMaYiM)—"and their union is from the Heavens" in *gematria* is the exact number corresponding to the combination of bride and groom—513 (ז = 6, ז = 7, ו = 6, ו = 6, ג = 3; מ = 40, נ = 50; ה = 5, ש = 300, מ = 40, י = 10, מ = 40 = 513).

KaLaH/ḤaTaN

BRIDE/GROOM

There are two Godly attributes that we as human beings must try to emulate. They represent the two different names in Hebrew for the Almighty. יהוה (Adonai) is God in His attribute of mercy. It has the feminine ending הָ, and our sages define it as מִדַּת הָרַחֲמִים (midat ha-raḥamim), the attribute of mercy, from the root word רֶחֶם (reḥem), or womb. אֱלֹהִים (Elohim) is the attribute of strict justice. That name has a masculine ending. It is God as the stern, strict ruler of the universe.

The world, in order to function, needs both male and female, even as it requires אֱלֹהִים (Elohim) and יהוה (Adonai). Without justice, there would be anarchy; without mercy and forgiveness, there would be destruction.

Two Hebrew words summarize these complementary ideals: חֶסֶד (ḥesed), mercy, and אֱמֶת (emet), truth. When Moses seeks to know God's essence, he is told that the Almighty is רַב חֶסֶד וֶאֱמֶת (rav ḥesed ve-emet), "abundant in goodness and truth" [Exodus 34:6].

In *gematria* חֶסֶד (HeSeD) and אֱמֶת (EMeT) total 513 (ח = 8, ס = 60, ד = 4; א = 1, מ = 40, ת = 400 = 513). Bring חָתָן (ḤaTaN) and כַּלָּה (KaLaH) together and their *gematria* as well is 513 (ח = 8, ת = 400, נ = 50; כ = 20, ל = 30, ה = 5 = 513).

Bride and groom together merge the two most important qualities of the Almighty.

חוּפָּה

HUPaH

CANOPY

The day of the wedding is a יוֹם גָּדוֹל (yom gadol), a great day.

In a far more profound sense, it is also the day when a child becomes גָּדוֹל (gadol)—mature and of age.

The Talmud discusses the difference between a קָטָן (katan), a minor, and a גָּדוֹל (gadol), someone who has reached the age of adulthood. The rabbis state that one who is סוֹמֵךְ עַל שֻׁלְחָן אָבִיו (someh al shulhan aviv), who relies on the table of his father, is still a minor. When he is סוֹמֵךְ עַל שֻׁלְחָן עַצְמוֹ (someh al shulhan azmo), when he is independent enough to rely upon his own table, that is, to feed himself and to provide for his own needs, he then becomes a גָּדוֹל (gadol).

Marriage means to set out on one's own.

עַל־כֵּן יַעֲזָב־אִישׁ אֶת־אָבִיו וְאֶת־אִמּוֹ וְדָבַק בְּאִשְׁתּוֹ
(Al ken ya'azov ish et aviv ve-et imo ve-davak be-ishto)

"Therefore shall a man leave his father and his mother and cleave unto his wife."

[Genesis 2:24]

The *gematria* of חוּפָּה (HUPaH) is 99 (ח = 8, ו = 6, פ = 80, ה = 5 = 99). The חוּפָּה (huppah) overhead proclaims the *gematria* of יוֹם גָּדוֹל (YOM GaDOL) (י = 10, ו = 6, מ = 40; ג = 3, ד = 4, ו = 6, ל = 30 = 99). This is a great day—when a person achieves the greatness of independence.

לָבָן

LaVaN

❧

WHITE

The bride wears a veil. It is to be white, לָבָן (lavan), as a symbol of purity.

Place different vowels under the word לָבָן (lavan) and it reads לְבֵן (le-ben), for a child. For the sake of modesty, the bride places a veil over her face. She ought no longer to be longed for or lusted after by others. But the very veil of purity and of modesty speaks to her groom with a different message. To her chosen one it says, "We will unite spiritually and physically." A significant purpose of marriage is not only our own happiness, but the creation of a family.

Under the wedding canopy there is already a "veiled" allusion to fulfillment of the מִצְוָה (mizvah) to "be fruitful and multiply."

הֲרֵי אַתְּ ...

HaReY AT...

BEHOLD, YOU ARE . . .

The words to be recited by the groom in conjunction with the placing of the ring upon the finger of the bride are the following:

הֲרֵי אַתְּ מְקֻדֶּשֶׁת לִי בְּטַבַּעַת זוּ כְּדַת מֹשֶׁה וְיִשְׂרָאֵל
(Harei at mekudeshet li be-taba'at zu ke-dat Mosheh
ve-Yisrael)

"Behold, you are consecrated to me with this ring according to the laws of Moses and of Israel."

[*Kiddushin* 5b]

Count the number of words in this phrase. They total nine. Tradition teaches us the significance of this number at the סֵדֶר (seder) table when we ask and answer:

תִּשְׁעָה מִי יוֹדֵעַ? תִּשְׁעָה אֲנִי יוֹדֵעַ. תִּשְׁעָה יַרְחֵי לֵדָה
(Tishah mi yode'a? Tishah ani yode'a Tishah yarḥei ledah)

"Who knows nine? I know nine. Nine are the months of pregnancy."

Marriage is a מִצְוָה (miẓvah) because it is the necessary legal prerequisite for fulfillment of the first divine commandment, פְּרוּ וּרְבוּ (peru u-revu)—be fruitful and multiply. The nine words that accompany the ring already allude to the hope that this union will result in the formation of a family.

Count the letters in the phrase. They total thirty-two. That is לֵב (lev)—the Hebrew word for heart. The declaration of marriage proposal comes with fullness of heart; the ring in its roundness conveys the hope that this love, like a circle, will be everlasting.

KiDUSHiYN

ENGAGEMENT/ SANCTIFICATION

The first stage of a Jewish marriage is called קִדּוּשִׁין (kidushin). No English word can do justice to its meaning.

Superficially, it corresponds to the English word *engagement*. Marriage is not yet complete. Bride and groom are joined together legally, but may not yet engage in sexual relations. Yet if they were to choose to dissolve their union even at this point, they would halachically require a divorce.

How can Jewish law consider them married and yet decree they may still not become intimate physically? Isn't the very meaning of marriage to bring two people together sexually? קִדּוּשִׁין (kidushin) proclaims that sex comes not as the first stage of marriage, but rather the last. Before husband and wife become intimate with their bodies, they must learn to relate on a level of קְדוּשָׁה (kedushah), holiness—the same root as קִדּוּשִׁין (kidushin)—to share values and outlooks, hopes and aspirations.

The *gematria* of קִדּוּשִׁין (KiDUSHiYN) is 470 (ק = 100, ד = 4, ו = 6, שׁ = 300, י = 10, ן = 50 = 470). That is identical to the *gematria* of כְּנַפְשֶׁךָ (Ke-NaFSHeKHa), as your own soul (כ = 20, נ = 50, פ = 80, שׁ = 300, כ = 20 = 470).

First make the commitment of קִדּוּשִׁין (kidushin). Be willing to treat your partner "as your own soul." Then proceed to the second stage of נִשּׂוּאִין (nisu'in), full marriage, with the assurance that true soul mates can now become full partners for life.

קִדּוּשִׁין
KiDUSHiYN

ENGAGEMENT/
SANCTIFICATION

A worthy mate is a divine blessing.

It is the fulfillment of one's fondest prayers. It is a divine response to the hopes of a lifetime.

But there is also an intangible, inexplicable, and undefinable other dimension at work.

The *gematria* of קִדּוּשִׁין (KiDUSHiYN) is 470 (ק = 100, ד = 4, ו = 6, שׁ = 300, י = 10, ן = 50 = 470). Do not hesitate to declare at the moment of קִדּוּשִׁין (kidushin)—כִּי יֵשׁ לוֹ מַזָּל טוֹב (KiY YeSH LO MaZaL TOV)—"that there is to him good fortune." The *gematria* of that observation, too, is 470 (כ = 20, י = 10; י = 10, שׁ = 300; ל = 30, ו = 6; מ = 40, ז = 7, ל = 30; ט = 9, ו = 6, ב = 2 = 470).

A man blessed with a good wife has מַזָּל (mazal) above all.

נְשׂוּאִין

NiSU'iYN

MARRIAGE

On the wedding day, bride and groom fast. The day of supreme happiness is also the day of supreme holiness.

True joy is not escape from reality. The שִׂמְחָה (simhah) of נְשׂוּאִין (nisu'in), marriage, is rooted in awareness of the seriousness of this moment.

The groom wears a *kittel*, the same garb with which man is clothed to meet his Maker after his death. Marriage asks us to think of the meaning of our lives to the very end of our days. It is to acknowledge that some day we will have to stand before our Creator in final judgment and give an accounting for the way in which we passed the days of our lives.

To what may a wedding day be compared, ask the sages. To יוֹם הַכִּפּוּרִים (Yom Ha-Kippurim) is the response, to the very Day of Atonement. Both demand introspection, commitment, seriousness of purpose. Both revolve around making the most important choices for the future. Bride and groom on this day are each to recite the lengthy confessional, the עַל חֵטְא (Al Het), which is part of the יוֹם כִּפּוּר (Yom Kippur) liturgy.

The *gematria* of נְשׂוּאִין (NiSU'iYN) is 417 (נ = 50, שׂ = 300, ו = 6, א = 1, י = 10, נ = 50 = 417). Its essence is shared with יוֹם הַכִּפּוּרִים (YOM Ha-KiPURYM), which also adds up to 417 (י = 10, ו = 6, מ = 40; ה = 5, כ = 20, פ = 80, ו = 6, ר = 200, י = 10, מ = 40 = 417).

After the Day of Atonement and after the day of the wedding, we begin a new life, forgiven for all past misdeeds, ready to face the future in purity and in holiness.

נִשׂוּאִין

NiSU'iYN

MARRIAGE

קִדּוּשִׁין (kidushin) is engagement. It is legally created with the transfer of an object of value from groom to bride, most usually the ring.

נִשׂוּאִין (nisu'in), full marriage, is affected by standing under the חוּפָּה (ḥuppah), the canopy. The canopy is a symbol not only of God overhead, but also of the "roof" above the couple who will soon share a home and the building up of a household.

Whatever the pressures of the outside world may be in the days ahead, marriage will afford the haven of home, the greatest blessing known to mankind. As Julius Hare so magnificently put it: "To Adam paradise was home. To the good among his descendants, home is paradise."

נִשׂוּאִין (NiSU'IYN) in *gematria* is 417 (נ = 50, שׂ = 300, ו = 6, א = 1, י = 10, ן = 50 = 417). What is the essence of marriage? הַבַּיִת (Ha-BaYiT), the home, which in *gematria* is also 417 (ה = 5, ב = 2, י = 10, ת = 400 = 417).

נְשׂוּאִין

NiSU'iYN

❦

MARRIAGE

All the letters of the Hebrew alphabet, according to the *Midrash*, came before God and pleaded with the Almighty to have the honor of being selected to start the words of the Torah.

Twenty-one of them were rejected. For one reason or another, they did not have sufficient merit for this great honor. The "winning contestant" proved to be the letter ב with which God began the Bible, as we read בְּרֵאשִׁית (bereshit), "in the beginning."

What is the uniqueness of the ב that allows it its preeminence above all other letters? The *Midrash* teaches, it is because the ב also begins the word בְּרָכָה (berakhah), which means blessing.

Understood on a more profound level, it is not simply because the ב is used at the start of yet another word that has a very positive connotation. Other letters serve the same function. It is rather that in its meaning as a number, ב equalling two, it defines the very essence of blessing. To be one alone, א, is the word for אָרוּר (arur), cursed. To be two is to know compassion and concern, to be able to express love and affection. ב , indeed, is בְּרָכָה (berakhah).

נְשׂוּאִין (nisu'in) is wedding. It has well been said that even the English word contains within it a fascinating insight: wedding is the moment when people learn to place "we" before "I." In Hebrew the *gematria* of נְשׂוּאִין (NiSU'IYN) is 417 (נ = 50, שׂ = 300, ו = 6, א = 1, י = 10, ן = 50 = 417). When two come together in true love, commitment, and holiness, that is לְסִימָן בְּרָכָה (le-siman berakhah) for a sign of blessing. The *gematria* of לְסִימָן בְּרָכָה (Le-SiYMaN BeRa-KHaH) is 417, identical to נְשׂוּאִין (NiSU'IYN) (ל = 30, ס = 60, י = 10, מ = 40, ן = 50; ב = 2, ר = 200, כ = 20, ה = 5 = 417).

עַד מֵאָה וְעֶשְׂרִים

AD Me'AH V'ESRiYM

UNTIL ONE HUNDRED
AND TWENTY

To young and to old, to bride and to groom, to every friend and member of the family, at a happy occasion, Jews convey the fond greeting עַד מֵאָה וְעֶשְׂרִים (ad me'ah v'esrim), until one hundred and twenty.

The greatest Jew who ever lived, מֹשֶׁה רַבֵּינוּ (Mosheh Rabeinu), Moses our Teacher, lived to that ripe old age. It becomes the goal for every one of us. To live longer than Moses is unthinkable. To reach his years is to be granted not only the great gift of length of days, but also the highest accolade of linkage with the life of the holiest one among our people.

The second paragraph of the שְׁמַע יִשְׂרָאֵל (Shema Yisrael), which we recite twice daily, concludes with the words

לְמַעַן יִרְבּוּ יְמֵיכֶם וִימֵי בְנֵיכֶם, עַל הָאֲדָמָה אֲשֶׁר נִשְׁבַּע יהוה לַאֲבֹתֵיכֶם לָתֵת
לָהֶם, כִּימֵי הַשָּׁמַיִם עַל־הָאָרֶץ
(Lema'an yirbu yemeikhem vi-mei veneikhem al ha-adamah
asher nishba Adonai la-avoteikhem latet lahem ki-mei
ha-shamayim al ha-arez)

"That your days may be multiplied and the days of your children upon the land which the Lord swore unto your fathers to give them as the days of the heavens above the earth."
[Deuteronomy 11:21]

For what length of time dare we hope that our "days be multiplied"? Consider the *gematria* of יְמֵיכֶם (YeMeYKHeM): י = 10, מ = 40, י = 10, כ = 20, ם = 40 = 120.

May we all deserve the divine blessing of length of days, "until one hundred and twenty"—and may the days all be happy as holidays—referred to in Hebrew as מוֹעֵד (MOED), whose *gematria*, too, is 120 (מ = 40, ו = 6, ע = 70, ד = 4 = 120).

Glossary

AMALEKITE	*Amalek*	עמלק
BAR MITZVAH/BAT MITZVAH	*Bar Miẓvah/Bat Miẓvah*	בר מצוה/בת מצוה
BEHOLD, YOU ARE . . .	*Harei At . . .*	הרי את . . .
BIRTH	*Leidah*	לידה
BITTER HERBS	*Maror*	מרור
BOOTH	*Sukkah*	סכה
BOY	*Yeled*	ילד
BRIDE	*Kallah*	כלה
CANDLE	*Ner*	נר
CANOPY	*Ḥuppah*	חופה
CIRCUMCISION	*Brit Milah*	ברית מילה
CITRON	*Etrog*	אתרג
COUNTING THE DAYS	*Sefirah*	ספירה
COVENANT/CIRCUMCISION	*Brit*	ברית
CUP	*Kos*	כוס
DARKNESS	*Ḥoshekh*	חשך
DAVID	*David*	דוד
DAY OF ATONEMENT	*Yom Ha-Kippurim*	יום הכפרים
DESERT	*Midbar*	מדבר
ELUL	*Elul*	אלול
ENGAGEMENT/ SANCTIFICATION	*Kidushin*	קדושין
EVERYTHING	*Kol*	כל
FESTIVAL OF BOOTHS	*Ḥag Ha-Sukkot*	חג הסוכות
FESTIVAL OF THE FIRST FRUITS	*Ḥag Ha-Bikkurim*	חג הבכורים
FESTIVAL OF FREEDOM	*Pesaḥ*	פסח
FESTIVAL OF LIGHTS	*Ḥanukkah*	חנוכה
FESTIVAL OF LOTS	*Purim*	פורים
FESTIVAL OF MATZOT	*Ḥag Ha-Maẓot*	חג המצות
FESTIVAL OF WEEKS	*Shavu'ot*	שבועות

FIFTH OF IYYAR	*He Iyyar*	ה׳ אייר
FISH	*Dag*	דג
FORGIVE	*Slaḥ*	סלח
FORTUNE/LUCK	*Mazal*	מזל
FREEDOM	*Ḥerut*	חרות
FROM ITS CANDLE	*Mi-Nerah*	מנרה
GIRL	*Yaldah*	ילדה
GROOM	*Ḥatan*	חתן
HAMAN	*Haman*	המן
I	*Anokhi*	אנכי
ISRAEL INDEPENDENCE DAY	*Yom Ha-Azma'ut*	יום העצמאות
JERUSALEM	*Yerushalayim*	ירושלים
JERUSALEM DAY	*Yom Yerushalayim*	יום ירושלים
JETHRO	*Yitro*	יתרו
JUDAH	*Yehudah*	יהודה
KING	*Melekh*	מלך
LAMENTATIONS	*Eikhah*	איכה
LEAVENING AGENT	*Se'or*	שאר
LETTERS ON THE DREIDEL	*Nun, Gimel, Shin, He*	נ, ג, ש, ה
LOT	*Pur*	פור
MACCABEE	*Maccabee*	מכבי
MANY	*Rabim*	רבים
MARRIAGE	*Nisu'in*	נשואין
MATITHIAS	*Matityahu*	מתתיהו
MATZAH	*Maẓah*	מצה
MAZEL TOV	*Mazal tov*	מזל טוב
MESSIAH	*Mashiaḥ*	משיח
MILK	*Ḥalav*	חלב
NAME	*Shem*	שם
NEW YEAR	*Rosh Ha-Shanah*	ראש השנה
NINTH OF AV	*Tishah Be-Av*	תשעה ב׳אב
OIL	*Ha-Shemen*	השמן
OUR FATHER, OUR KING	*Avinu Malkeinu*	אבינו מלכנו
PALM TREE	*Lulav*	לולב
PARDON	*Meḥal*	מחל
PASSOVER	*Pesaḥ*	פסח

REJOICING	Oneg	ענג
SABBATH	Shabbat	שבת
SATAN	Ha-Satan	השטן
SCROLL	Megillah	מגלה
SEPARATION	Havdalah	הבדלה
SINAI	Sinai	סיני
SIXTH DAY	Yom Ha-Shishi	יום הששי
SPICES	Besamim	בשמים
SPRING	Aviv	אביב
STORY	Haggadah	הגדה
TISHREI	Tishrei	תשרי
TWENTY-EIGHTH DAY OF IYYAR	Khof Ḥet Iyyar	כ״ח אייר
UNTIL ONE HUNDRED AND TWENTY	Ad Me'ah ve-Esrim	עד מאה ועשרים
WEEPING	Bekhi	בכי
WHITE	Lavan	לבן
WINE	Yayin	יין
YOU SHALL DWELL	Teshvu	תשבו
ZION	Ẓiyon	ציון

Index

ABOUT THE AUTHOR

Benjamin Blech has been Rabbi of Young Israel of Oceanside, New York, for over three decades, and he is Assistant Professor of Talmud at Yeshiva University in New York City. He has served as Scholar-in-Residence in numerous congregations throughout the United States and Canada and has lectured to Jewish communities in Israel, Australia, and many other countries.

Rabbi Blech has written articles for *Tradition*, *Jewish Life*, *Reader's Digest*, *Jewish Week*, and *Newsday*. He is the author of *The Secrets of Hebrew Words* and *Understanding Judaism: The Basics of Deed and Creed*.